Consciousness and the Aconscious in Psychoanalytic Theory

Consciousness and the Aconscious in Psychoanalytic Theory

Ahmed Fayek, PhD

ROWMAN & LITTLEFIELD
Lanham • Boulder • New York • London

Published by Rowman & Littlefield
A wholly owned subsidiary of The Rowman & Littlefield Publishing Group, Inc.
4501 Forbes Boulevard, Suite 200, Lanham, Maryland 20706
www.rowman.com

16 Carlisle Street, London W1D 3BT, United Kingdom

British Library Cataloguing in Publication Information Available

Library of Congress Cataloging-in-Publication Data

Fayek, Ahmed.
Consciousness and the aconscious in psychoanalytic theory / Ahmed Fayek.
pages cm.
Includes bibliographical references and index.
ISBN 978-1-4422-4250-0 (cloth : alk. paper) -- ISBN 978-1-4422-4252-4 (electronic)
1. Consciousness. 2. Psychoanalysis. I. Title.
BF311.F365 2014
153--dc23
2014025323

™ The paper used in this publication meets the minimum requirements of American National Standard for Information Sciences Permanence of Paper for Printed Library Materials, ANSI/NISO Z39.48-1992.

Printed in the United States of America

To

Mostatfa

Aminah

Amirah

Table of Contents

Introduction

If we tell an ordinary educated person that there is great debate going on now among a wide range of thinkers, neurologists, and psychologists about defining "consciousness" and explaining it, we will likely get a response of astonishment. Consciousness does not constitute a problem of any sort to the average person. How come it is then getting such attention in contemporary circles of serious, knowledgeable, and previously unrelated groups of professionals?

In an interesting exploration of the concept of the "mind," Johnson (2003) suggests that the evolution of the mind is the product of two sudden achievements by the human race: the attainment of language that led to the birth of symbolic thinking and a major adjustment to that acquired tool of thinking in the pre-Socratic era, when the Greek thinkers invented, or discovered, abstract ideas and thus were able to think objectively. In a way, Johnson considered the mind a separate event in the evolution of the human race, in the sense that consciousness evolves in tandem with the evolution of the human species, but the mind was a product of those two events. Thus, the mind could be seen as an entity with a teleological nature of its own. We could therefore consider the emergence of consciousness, as an issue, at the present time just the contribution of the mind in the evolution of consciousness. Johnson's idea that history is the creator of the mind is not controversial, but it needs to be looked at beyond the words used in his postulate. Whatever the stand we take regarding such a notion, we cannot ignore what Cicero said: "The man who has no idea of what happened before he was born always remains a child" (in Johnson, 2003).

Therefore, I would like to condense a history of the evolution that materialized in the phenomenon of the mind in a few paragraphs, to show that the mind has been the manifestation of quantitative changes in consciousness that turned into a few qualitative leaps. I would like to do that to underline that our contemporary interest in consciousness is the expected outcome of the major philosophical endeavours of Western thinking, of which psychoanalysis is a stage in its progression. Consciousness, as an issue in its own right, could not possibly materialize if psychoanalysis did not demonstrate the existence of the unconscious and the "aconscious" alongside all conscious activities. Consciousness changed from something that explains to something that needs to be explained.

Human consciousness, the most distinct feature in the mutation that resulted in creating our species, changed the ways of communication between the members of the species, that is, it turned the vocal sounds and bodily gestures into languages. The slow and gradual recognition of the regularity of messaging to each other—the basis of language—gave birth to speech and talking. However, our history shows that changes happen to us before we recognize their happening. Once humans recognized that they had language to use in "talking" to each other, they noticed that they were distinct from the rest of the animal kingdom, and they were also different from each other (Ford 1963). It took some time before recognizing that the constituents of the language (words) could be written. Writing gave birth to civilization as the next human invention. The evolution of human consciousness caused new recognitions that, when developed, became the human mind—the part of the personal consciousness that could be shared with others.

In the occidental civilizations[1] (Acadian, Samarian, Assyrian, Babylonian, and Egyptian), consciousness was originally used to organize the state and turn the myths about the origins of things into religions (Solomon and Higgens, 1996). But gradually some individuals started to pose questions about the current ideas and beliefs, and a new breed of individuals appeared in the societies. They were what were later called philosophers. If we jump a few thousand years to the age of the professional philosopher in the Greek civilization we will notice that philosophers were—from the beginning—addressing two basic issues: nature and its roots on one side, and the conditions of human life as part of the social network (ibid.). It is interesting that those two issues progressed to constitute an *intrinsic* duality in all of the fields of philosophy since its inception and characterized philosophical thinking till now (Edwards 1972; Hendrich 2005; Russell 1967). The pre-Socratic philosophers changed "philosophy" from man's dealing with the immediate and concrete to the abstracts of his concerns. The abstract dealings with nature and living made philosophers take the human subject as the philosophical subject; his consciousness, knowledge, and conceptions of the matters around him were not only of philosophical importance, but he who owned those attributes became a central issue in their debates.

Thales—the early Greek thinker—started the search for "logical thinking" when he asked: how could I discover if the statement I hear is correct or false? (Gottlieb 2002; Johnson 2003). The need for logic was born and the post-Socratic Greek philosophers generated logical arguments and created a branch of consciousness that deals with logic as an inherent constituent of our speech. The Socratic and the post-Socratic thinkers argued about the human subject, speculated about his nature and the nature of his existence, and Aristotle tried to itemize knowledge and write about it separately. Philosophy reached a stage of maturity that made it stand out as the organizer of knowledge—not only as its manifestation. There were a few centuries when philosophy dealt with a new product of human consciousness—Christianity—where duality was divided between Man and his Creator. However, human consciousness came back to be its main subject: Man as part of nature and as a conscious being. The pose of the medieval period resulted in two major additions to philosophy: scholastic, or organized, methods of dealing with the subject matters of the arguments, and the principles of interpretation. A duality of body and soul arose from a great deal of debating because there was supposedly a holy "text" to consult in that matter. Yet, there were no easy agreements between the debaters on the meanings in the text. Therefore, group debates and trends in interpretation resulted in highlighting the importance of the methodological approaches to the issues debated. Not only did that lead to perfecting the scholarly methods but created schools of thought (Edwards 1972; Gilson 1991; Reese 1999). The budding interest in morality and human nature that were practical issues in Greek philosophy became main issues in Christianity. They puzzled about a gap between consciousness and its dictates on will—the gap between consciousness and moral issues including aesthetics and passions. This gap had its origin in the problems of "sin" but gradually changed into a gap between mind and body.

Descartes expounded that gap to investigate the problem of self- knowledge through dialectics of certainty and uncertainty (Descartes in Clarke 2000; Descartes in Copleston 1993). A religious hint in this argument could be sensed in the subtle link he established between consciousness and personal responsibility. The brain was not yet a subject for serious study but the notion of the mind created a new duality: consciousness and consciousness of consciousness. The transcendence of consciousness became the most central and intriguing philosophical argument in Western culture. Over the years, the philosophical investigation of the transcendence of consciousness led to a gradual acknowledgment of a missed ring in the link between mind and consciousness. Leibniz acknowledged the existence of bodily perceptions that are faint to be conceived by the mind to become conscious (Leibniz in Antognazza 2009; Leibniz in Copleston 1993). Shelling considered the unconscious an entity that is part of a process leading to consciousness (Limnatis 2008). Schopenhauer (in Berman and Berman 1995) had a conception of unconsciousness that was the closest to Freud's concept of the id, which Freud associated with the unconscious.

The philosophers who came to the concept of the unconscious did that when they sensed or encountered a basic absent link in the transcendence of consciousness. They realized that the transcendence of consciousness does not account for an intriguing phenomena: the inadequacy of consciousness to explain all of knowledge; there is knowledge that comes to being without the participation of consciousness. Shedding their limiting interests for matters of pure epistemology and metaphysics steered the philosophers' attention to the discoveries in both nomothetic and idiographic sciences. Both branches of science came up with major discoveries about consciousness, and the philosophers realized that they have things to say about those discoveries, as they have much to say about their own endeavors.

Neurologists had a different stance when it came to investigating consciousness. It always made sense to them to consider consciousness a function of the brain, because the brain is the only organ in the body that could tell us if the person is conscious or not. This is a simplistic way of saying that the brain is the organ of consciousness. Neurology achieved vast and impressive gains in the fields of anatomy and physiology of the brain, and the rest of the nervous system. In the past few decades *observing* brain activity in response to certain demands put on the subject—through innovative equipment and methods—has increased, expanded, refined, and given very concrete explanatory insights. Although there are reservations in different theories to that conception, we have yet to find another way to identify the bodily organ that could house and *process* consciousness.

Notwithstanding, all those investigations were neural quantitative observations but did not provide an answer to Bertrand Russell's well-known question: how do qualia emerge from merely neural activity? (in Velmans 2009). This question is about a needed leap from quantitative knowledge to qualitative comprehension of consciousness; a leap that keeps eluding neurology till now. In terms of the anatomy and physiology of the nervous system there is very little still *missing* that needs to be found, yet big enough to provide a neurological solution to the problem of consciousness soon. There seems to be something *lacking* in the neurological project that has to be incorporated in the search for the basis of consciousness.

Psychology, the science of the conscious phenomena *par excellence,* studies it and makes impressive strides in its detailed "description" of its manifestations. The experimental model in psychology enriched the explorations of many aspects of consciousness like thinking and memory, and made possible exploring the dynamic interaction of those components and its role in the formation of the personality of the subject. However, there were two obstacles in the way of psychology to be tackled before consciousness itself. Psychology studies consciousness via its cognitive output, thus it has a slanted view of its core nature due to the indirectness of its model of investigation. Cognition is not purely conscious and an important aspect of it is noncognitive, like intuitive thinking and emotional distortions. Some major parts of the mental processes take place outside of consciousness. They could not be defined in exact ways to gauge their participation in consciousness.

In psychology, methodology requires more adapting of the subject matter of the research to the experimental model, because the experimental mode is controlled by the means of expressing its results. We are always conscious of "something"; even the absence of an expected cognitive matter is a cognitive state that is studied in psychology. Adapting consciousness to the experimental model involves turning it into behavioural or quasi-behavioral forms like perceptions, so that the investigation could be set up in experimental modality of *independent* and *dependant* factors. Abiding by those "scientific" demands forces psychology to study the reflection of consciousness on certain manifestations of its existence, but fails to get to its source. Psychology recognizes that it misses the personal aspect of consciousness in that approach, and is quite aware that "the subjective" attribute of consciousness has to be sacrificed in that way of examining it. Psychology studies consciousness without the conscious-subject. The interest in studying the "person-ality," which took off strongly in the fifties and sixties of the last century, led to a similar impasse: a person without his consciousness. All the efforts made to study personality through perception or to study perception through the person came to the same point: something is missing that makes the matching between the two factors questionable.

The confluence of the interests and discoveries in the three camps of philosophy, neurology, and psychology were all meeting at a new point regarding the human being. The common shared interest in consciousness was because consciousness was a *metaphor* for the human being. Philosophers became intrigued by those discoveries for their possible links with matters of ontology, logic, the nature of the mind, and new branches of knowledge, like language. Those issues were promising a new conception of the human subject. Neurologists found some useful conceptions of mind-body issues in the work of the philosophers of the last three centuries. Psychologists were interested in the ability of new neurology to specify neural activities associated with mental activities. But, they found that the common denominator they all share was the *phenomenon of human consciousness*. Human consciousness, the common denominator among those inclined people, changed from the tool of research into the subject matter of research. In a different but revealing way, consciousness became the subject matter that deserves looking into after being, up until now, the way to look at matters.

The difficulties encountered in studying consciousness by the philosopher, the neurologist, and the psychologist lead to realizing that *there is more to consciousness than what we are able to grasp and have a hold of.* Although all of those researchers came to the same realization from different directions, they could not agree on what could complement the picture. The philosopher wondered about the transcendence of consciousness and if the answer could be exploring that phenomenon more. The neurologists suggested different reformulations to account for the limitations of their endeavors, but they were mainly about making distinctions between two types of consciousnesses. Psychologists called it the unconscious (possibly emboldened by Freud's usage of the term).

The agreement that consciousness is not comprehensive enough to explain everything about it leads us to a serious query: is there something lacking in consciousness or is it something missing? If consciousness is missing something like one of its qualifications then we have to look for it somewhere else, for example, a way to relate it to its quality, or to think of different degrees of intensities. But if consciousness is lacking something, the lack would be in the subject himself. Consciousness separate from the conscious-subject could be incomprehensive because when we bring the subject into *his* experience of consciousness he would undoubtedly have what could complete it to us. A person might feel scared of something on the floor that looks like a snake, but his conscious experience discovers non-movement and the fear subsides. Lack of movement identifies what is present, and its absence is a lack in what is not a snake. A lack is a gap that is sometimes difficult to define, but impossible to false-step. What lacks in consciousness is undefinable but not unidentifiable, because what is present determines what is lacking. Consciousness of the external world could be insufficient, distorted, and inaccurate because something lacking is defined as missing.

Consciousness of oneself is different. If consciousness of oneself is distorted, or limited, neither the person himself nor the "other" would be able to know what is lacking. A lack in consciousness of self appears unrelated to the subject's conscious experience. A phobic person would know that his fear of snakes is not related or conditional on seeing a snake. His phobia of snakes is there all the time; not related to seeing, a possible encounter with one, or to anything particular about them is a possible actual danger. The unreasonable fear of snakes points to a lack in the subject's reasoning that constructs his consciousness fear.

That lack was referred to as the un-conscious. However, the unconscious in that sense was merely the *negation* (un-) of consciousness. It was not something explainable but just a simple way of giving the lack a term to define it.

Freud was the first thinker-investigator who approached the issue of the unconscious head on. He first considered it an entity in its own right that could be reached if we manage to inactivate consciousness by hypnosis. He strove to study it as an absent aspect of consciousness that could be made present—something missing, not lacking. He resolutely dedicated himself to forming a theory of the missing consciousness, that is, the unconscious. This approach could have been acceptable as a discovery, even if it had not led to a comprehensive theory of consciousness. The unconsciousness was repressed consciousness, therefore, rationally and in hindsight, the missing consciousness due to repression should have solved the problem of consciousness as it stood then. The unconscious, within an incomprehensive theory of consciousness, was enough to complement the missing knowledge of the conscious. However, Freud was aspiring (mostly unconsciously) to formulate a comprehensive theory of the subject; conscious, unconscious, and both.

Freud's renowned and celebrated concept of the unconscious as a function of the mechanism of repression proved to be insufficient to offer a solution to his aspiration to have a comprehensive theory of the subject. There were two reasons for that: neglecting his *Project for a Scientific Psychology*, a work he wrote in 1895 and was missing until discovered in 1950. The second is the beginning of psychoanalysis with the treatment of hysteria through hypnosis.

Freud was almost done with his studies on hysteria when he—a neurologist through and through—took on a new *Project*: writing *a scientific psychology for the neurologist*. The *Project* is a unique document. When Freud was almost finished with the *Project*, he shelved it. It was discovered and published in 1950 as if it was the last of his works, when it was, in fact, his first. The *Project*—as we will see in chapter four—is remarkable in an unusual way. There is a major disagreement among the scholars of psychoanalysis on whether the *Project* was a psychological or a neurological document. However, there is almost a total agreement that it had all the portents of a major psychological theory, which was to become the whole theory of psychoanalysis. Better, the argument about the nature of that project reflects a core problem we face now about the proper approach to studying consciousness: should we approach it from the side of psychology and the subject to move to the brain and the mind or should we start from the brain to the mind then to the subject? Moreover, Freud's deep interest in writing this *Project* (Freud, 20 October 1895) and then the sudden loss of interest, though kept it until it was discovered, mirrors the same ambivalence the scholars still have about how to approach consciousness.

Damasio wrote a book entitled *Self Comes to Mind* (2012). Using the *double entendre* of the title he gave an explicit and relatively detailed view of the neural foundation of the sense of self and its evolution, which makes the self find a place in the mind. The book could be called neurology for the psychologists. Freud's *Project*—more than a century before—was supposed to be the reverse, but it turned out to be the same; a neurology for the psychologist; but he put it aside.[2] With all the meaning of the word, fortunately Freud embarked on discovering the psychology of the subject, hence psychoanalysis was born.

Freud's discarding of the *Project* was a blessing in disguise. Because it contained the complete model of psychoanalysis in an embryonic form, it took Freud forty-four years more to unfold that theory completely. He provided in the *Project* the main points, issues, and problems entailed in a theory of the subject. He searched for the psychology of the subject in clinical experience, complimented with a rich cultural background, sharp insights, and a remarkable intuitive mind. His long journey in that endeavor is documented in thorough detail, showing how he learned without any predetermined plan, but by only a preliminary roadmap. If he had known in 1895 that he had discovered the core idea of psychoanalysis, the theory might not have reached us in the way that allowed *learning from its gradual formulation, and still keep learning till now*. We learned a way of thinking more than substantive facts; a main distinctive feature of psychoanalysis. Jones says: "Nowhere in Freud's published writings do we find such brilliant example of his capacity for abstruse thought and sustained close reasoning" (1954, 420). In other words, Freud discarded the *Project* when it was, in fact, his first step in the journey to discovering psychoanalysis. He did not realize that it was the first part of his endeavor, and not knowingly continued what has already begun, but neglected.

Freud's speculative enterprise in the *Project* with its heavy neurological terminology succeeded in masking the psychological fabric of the text. Now that we have the whole theory developed—though not fully or sufficiently articulated (see Fayek 2013)—we can go back to the *Project* and read it as a psychological text. What I mean is that we can now replace Freud's symbols, abbreviations, and physical concepts that he used in the *Project* with psychological ones and discover that the *Project* was the kernel of a theory of the subject. Most importantly, it is a theory of the *aconscious* and the birth of consciousness from it. Sperry (1975), a neurologist who introduced and used the term emergence to explain consciousness as a phenomenon that comes from another, approves an essential of that theory of the aconscious. He averred that consciousness is not a separate psychical entity that emerges from independent and separate processes, or a distinct entity that could be annexed to other psychical entities; consciousness is a modification in the function of aconsciousness.

The modification that gives birth to consciousness is a process that could explain major differences between our consciousness and consciousness in other animals. The manner by which aconsciousness evolves during the life of the individual and allows consciousness to emerge and entwine with it opens our eyes to something very specific about human consciousness. *Human consciousness could become sick although there is no criterion for its health.*

The treatment of hysteria began with using hypnosis with patients, ostensibly to circumvent the patients' passion to talk about themselves and symptoms and to make them talk about something else. Hypnosis allowed Freud a closer look at psychical material that became *un*-"consciousd" because it was expelled from consciousness (for different conscious reasons). Retrieving that material by hypnosis revealed the place this material had in consciousness before. Hypnosis revealed that the retrieved material could not be considered merely forgotten consciousness, but a deliberate forgetfulness. The unconscious was not a distinct entity; it was merely a *reversed* conscious state. It would have been better to call the repressed non-conscious to avoid concealing its origin in consciousness. Nonetheless, when Freud abandoned hypnosis and relied on the patient's free associations, he realized that the concept of unconsciousness is misleading. Gradually he discovered aspects of unconsciousness that required redefining it. He formulated three meanings of unconsciousness. The first was continuation of the original meaning of repressing unacceptable conscious thoughts, urges, memories, etc., and it was an adjectival meaning of unconsciousness. He coined the term dynamic unconsciousness to point to the interplay of psychical forces that keep some conscious material out or allowing them back in. The third meaning was material that does not have the attributes that allow it to become conscious. He designated it as systemically unconscious or true aconsciousness (I suggest calling it aconscious for reasons that will come later).

NOTES

1. I am not sure enough of my understanding of the oriental civilizations of east of the Euphrates to discuss the place of consciousness in them.

2. Freud started with the opposite intention that Damasio had and ended up with what Damasio intended. Does his shelving the *Project* say something about Damasio's point of view?

Chapter One

Consciousness

Two Faces of a Puzzle

When we are conscious we know that decidedly and without need for proofs to the fact. Even in waking up from sleep (which has its particular state of consciousness) we become aware of the change in our state of mind, which we all associate with consciousness. More evidently, when we see someone coming out of a state of non-consciousness we recognize the difference right away. Better, it seems that we know consciousness even from its opposite; non-consciousness.

Yet, the literature on consciousness and the related studies of cognitive functions is replete with definitions of that evident condition. There are many disagreements and "points of view" in those definitions that turn consciousness into a puzzle. Anthony (2002) raises a pertinent question: is consciousness a concept or a meaning? This question has two correct answers, but neither leads to a conclusive definition of consciousness. Larmand (1996) notices that there is no uniformal agreement on consciousness because thinkers do not usually agree on the types of consciousnesses they are talking about. Becerra (2004) confirms that there is too many meanings to the word consciousness and too many words for the phenomenon of consciousness. Bickard (2005) considers the concept of representation crucial in defining consciousness, but it is in itself a concept open for all sorts of meanings. Sloman (quoted in Velmans 2009) says: "people who discuss consciousness delude themselves in thinking that they know what they are talking about." Velmans (2009) adds: "the term means many different things to many different people, and no universally agreed upon 'core meaning' exists. This is strange because we each have 'psychological data' about what it is like to *be conscious* or to *have consciousness* to serve as the basis for an agreed definition" (1). From the looks of it in the literature, consciousness is a puzzle. But is consciousness the puzzle or is it the way we deal with it that turns it into a puzzle?

The literature displays more interest in the nature of consciousness; maybe as the means to understanding *what it is to be conscious!* The most important outcome of this seemingly chaotic literature is a subtle blurring of the boundaries between *consciousnesses as a puzzle and puzzling about being conscious.* All the efforts in the course of identifying and defining consciousness seem to lead to two issues that are not dealt with separately, so we can identify their groupings in the literature easily: *What is particular about the state of consciousness that puzzles?* and *How does that state generate*? The responses to those two issues are dispersed within the abundance of the literature and share the thinkers disproportionately.

It is thus difficult, and maybe counterproductive, to present a comprehensive review of the literature on the subject, because it comprises a great variety of visions, particularly in the area of methodology. Moreover, the abundance of work and the parallel abundance of views give the impression that there is a missed link in the matter and that would distract from the subject of consciousness itself. In spite of the distinct labelling of the different schools in the field it is noticeable that delineating the subtle distinctions between them is not quite decisive. Choosing an angle to sort out and categorize the rich discussions in the literature is unavoidable, though it is likely to be arbitrary. My choice is to address two identified issues that occupy the thinkers of the subject in their own distinct ways: *why* does consciousness originate, and *what* originates when it does. The first category of thinkers answers the first question. It considers consciousness a product or a *function* of the brain, thus it is called the functional school, though it also goes by other names that correspond to the basic premise in the answer like the materialist and the physicalists. The main premise of this school is offering a material origin—the brain—as the generator of consciousness. It answers the first question of *why* consciousness originates by saying: *conciseness happens because of brain activity.*

The starting point of the second approach is identifying the phenomenon of consciousness first and then provides the neurologist with what to look for in brain activities. It believes that basic features in consciousness, which seems to be beyond brain activities and if not clearly stipulated therefore the neurologist, would either ignore them or miss something in brain activity that could be a manifestation of those features. This school, called the phenomenalist, centers its inquiries around the structure of conscious experiences, or on consciousness as a phenomenon that requires attention before limiting it to the avidity of an origin.

THE TWO MAIN SCHOOLS OF THOUGHT

A. *The Functionalists*

The Functionalists consider consciousness a function of brain activity, and see no other possible *explanation* to it. Their methodological argument is that the brain is the only organ in the body that could engender consciousness. They do not contend with the reporting of the individual's reporting of his experiences of consciousness, because it is likely that it will include aspects of consciousness that do fit within the boundaries of brain activity. They confine (prefer) their studies to the aspects of the phenomena that could be examined by a "third party"; phenomena that render themselves to examination by a scientific method or machine. Third-party definition comes from the inherent rejection of self-reporting of consciousness (first party) or scientists' or others' observations (second party), because they would be tainted with *subjectivity*. The functionalists exclude subjectivity from their work and seek objective measurable manifestations of brain activity. Reducing conscious activity and its cognitive aspects (mental) to physical brain activity that indicates its happening makes—or actually forces—the functionalists to exclude some basic stipulations of consciousness. It has to be emphasized that even if this logic is accepted as a general rule, it is founded on excluding the mental phenomena or its manifestations that do not relate to material originated in the brain.

Dennett says (1983): "[consciousness] arises when there is work for it to do" (384). However, consciousness is mental activity that never ceases in waking life or sleep, and is always about something whether physical or personal. Moreover, the functionalists have no material (neurological) explanation of the quality of consciousness (Qualia). If we have the most sophisticated means to map the anatomical and neurological activity of the brain of someone admiring a painting we would still not find where, when, and what that admiration was generated in the brain. Therefore, some functionalists presume that the quality is simply an attribute of the painting and the brain is responding to its existence in the physical world. In other terms, part of perceiving quality is because it is interwoven in the external material world and the brain is capable of responding to it as integral entities of the stimuli.

A branch of this main trend examined some specific characteristics in human consciousness, which challenge those views. There is no neurological explanation—in those strict terms—to the ability to think symbolically or the usage of language. The theoretical proposition of that school still remained purely materialistic: if consciousness and its cognitive manifestations are functions of the brain we therefore should expect to find the roots of our consciousness in the brains of higher primates, because their brains are similar to ours, be it smaller in size. The logic behind this proposition is that if the difference between human and mammalian brains is restricted to matters of size, it could be said that the qualitative distinction of human consciousness is only an evolution of rudimentary roots or beginnings in the brains of primates; therefore they still should be included in the general activity of the brain.

There is overriding understanding that evolution has only one direction, which is toward the improvement of the species. This understanding made thinkers, neurologists, and psychologist consider human consciousness an advancement of a lower kind of brains, due to morphological and neurological improved capabilities of the human organ of the brain. Even thinkers like Dennett, who gave language a prominent distinct place in his valuation of consciousness, still treated it as an "advantageous characteristic" that has a location in the brain, but did not recognize its specific and particular role in structuring consciousness, that is, it is as any other function of the brain, yet has an additional organizing role of affecting other brain functions.

Functional thinking, in general is *deductive*, which is the general methodology of physical sciences. It seeks knowledge in examining cause-effect relations; seeking cause for certain effects (like consciousness). This approach starts from the details of the observed aiming at reaching (deducing) a general guiding rule that integrates the details in one comprehensive conception. The basic principle in deductive thinking is functionality or causality. A functional relationship is enough for the functionalist to explain the subject matter of the observed subject; it is to some extent a pragmatic ontology. Once relations between the brain as cause and consciousness as its function or effect has been determined, objective measures to studying this relation further are meant to give better explanations. Subjectivity is rejected because it requires and invokes more than one explanation. Cause-effect relations reveal links that is adequate to explaining them. Subjectivity could see in a phenomenon more than what meets the eye, thus it opens the gate to the possibility that what seems to be the cause or the effect might be eluding the observer. Moreover, subjective observations require interpreting the links, not just explaining them, and that compounds the problem of subjectivity.

There are critics of aspiring for absolute objectivity in the study of consciousness and believe that subjectivity, or some of it, is inevitable. They provide solid arguments, which de Sousa (2002) summarises in saying: "The claim is that persons differ from all other things in that they cannot be exhaustively described in the third person. Any attempt to do so will fail to capture something about every human being that is *essentially subjective*." de Sousa's position from that argument is that subjectivity is not a unitary concept, anyhow. Therefore, he questions the value of raising it as a discrediting notion of objectivity. So, when subjectivity is considered in criticizing the functionalists for ignoring it, the inadequacy of being definite about what the terms really mean will show the weakness of the phenomenalists'[1] stand, and will remove it from being an obstacle in the way of the physicalists.

Including cognitive sciences in the search for a definition of consciousness opened the scope of theorising, and changed the points of emphasis in the functional school. With cognition to contend with the functionalists conceded that consciousness is a *situated* activity, which meant that it needs more than a direct simple neurological explanation. Cognitive processes happen within a defined task that has definite inputs and outputs. While cognitive processes are active a flow of perceptual information continues to feedback and that affects processing, producing activities that could influence the environment that pertains to the cognitive tasks. Thus, cognition with the accompanying consciousness is not just a function of the brain; it is a complex and dynamic *mental* event that involves other organs with their own input in the neural event. Consciousness, therefore, is an active process, situated, and embodied, and acts as an embedded facility that includes the continual interactions of the body with the external world.

The novelty in that development is considering cognition as a process that happens *only* if coupled to the external world. Accordingly, the notion of an intermediate process (representation) between the external and the internal world could not be discarded, since the feedback is active all the time. The proposed internal representations, which are essential and central in studying phenomenal consciousness, are explained by the functionalists as evolutionary gains that are basically of material source, and that cognition is an activity that comprises the body, the environment, and the brain. Consciousness became a very complicated issue not just a complex subject, because the notions of mental representation and internal activities decoupled from the environment remained unanswered. However, this novelty in looking at consciousness did not address the fact that the *mind* could think abstractly too, which means that it does not depend on the external or the internal stimulation to function. It also generates artistic entities, and has the ability to deal with its own activity; all that is beyond a materialistic explanation. We are back to the old problem that faced the classical functionalists, be it from a different angle. The functionalists were looking for a match between brain activities and consciousness, whether by discarding what does not fit, or winding the material source to comprise more of its attributes.

It becomes clear, in the context of identifying the epistemological bases of functional thinking, that functionalism would face two major problems. The first is its inability to explain brain activities that are not conscious but are necessary and actively contributing to consciousness (Edelman & Tononi 2001; Damasio 2004; Blackmore 2005). The second, is the aspects of consciousness that do not produce specific neurological manifestations that could be measured by a third party, like the quality of conscious experiences and the wide range of abstract and symbolic thinking.

B. The Phenomenalists

The insufficient neurological explanation of all aspects of consciousness invited another school of thought to engage in studying consciousness differently. This school is the phenomenalist school. Phenomenological philosophy, established by Edmund Husserl (1859-1938), was active in the early twentieth century. It was the philosophy of bracketing the existent phenomena to analyze them out of any context they exist in, in order to reach their essence.[2] The phenomenological school of studying consciousness advocated the search for its essence not its material origin. Its thinkers, who believed in the subjective feature of consciousness, advocated bracketing it and studying it as a phenomenon of whether those features are neurologically viable to third-party investigation or only reportable by a first person as experience, or observed by a second person as events. Phenomenalism, deals with the phenomena of consciousness first, not hampered primarily by the burden of proof.

The phenomenalists' approach accepts the involvement of the brain in generating consciousness. However, in the example of admiring a painting the phenomenalist does not accept that beauty is a material attribute of the painting that the brain could perceive or conceive. Beauty to the phenomenalist is purely phenomenal and not a product of the brain; there should be another explanation to it rather than assuming that it was a product of the brain. The phenomenalist rejects reducing the quality of consciousness or its subjectivity to merely neural activity, because there are people who could appreciate the material world and others who could only respond to it mechanistically. Despite the general similarity of the two brains, one would see beauty and the other not. Moreover, if there are some qualitative aspects in the perceived world that the brain could turn into qualia like symmetry, proportionality, and harmony, no purely neurological explanation could cover the conscious content that comes with the conceived qualia, such as liking or disliking the perceived.

The phenomenalist sees consciousness to have features that go beyond the functionalist's neural explanations. Velmans puts it very succinctly when he says (2009): "When consciousness is present, *phenomenal content* (consciousness of something) is present. Conversely, when phenomenal content is absent conscious is absent" (4). What Velmans is implicitly saying is that it is not enough to assume that the brain generates consciousness, because the brain does not generate *all* of consciousness, and consciousness has to be complimented by having content, else it would not be consciousness. Those arguments imply a difference between the first person reporting of consciousness, and a third person's account of observing the neural manifestations of consciousness. The phenomenalist argues that the quality and content of consciousness have no material equivalent for the third person to report; or the third-party account of consciousness does not have the means to include everything that characterizes it. Thus, third-party observations run short of including any subjective appreciation of the content of consciousness.

Furthermore, consciousness engages any situation and formulae a subjective view of it. Even when the person is asked of his opinion and he does not have one he realizes that absence consciously, meaning that it is usual for one to have an opinion. The difference of opinions about some material-subject in the external world could not be explained by the differences between two brains forming those opinions. The problem for the functionalist is the existence of the subjective contribution to *any* conscious experiences, whatever the nature or degree of subjectivity (maybe this is what de Sousa [2002] argued).

Phenomenalists rely on an ostensive definition of mindfulness that includes and excludes certain related and unrelated phenomena of awareness. The definition considers the experience that deserves to be called conscious and defines it accordingly. Consciousness can be (happen) without any external input and without any output to the external world. As such, despite the fact that such mental activity would have accompanying neural manifestations it is still neurologically unexplainable. As this happens all the time then consciousness is not coupled completely or all the time to a physiological event like neural activity. A person could sense musical tunes, for instance, and visualize images that goes with it (Beethoven's Moon Light Sonata got its name that way). *If the brain could initiate its own activity—link a vision to a sound—it loses its status as* the *organ of transforming stimuli into neural activity because it becomes like any other organ that engenders stimulation.* There is room in consciousness for the particularity of the complexities of cognition and its quality. What is more specific about phenomenal consciousness is that it comprises *consciousness of consciousness*; consciousness could transcend itself and become a mental product as well as the mental tool. As we will discuss in the next chapter, neural feedback could explain the physiology of transcendence but not the metaphysics of the neural loop.

Phenomenal consciousness accounts for the phenomenon itself and the phenomenalists do not constrain themselves by the limitations of accounting for all what is involved in consciousness. If the neurologists have no explanation for the transcendence of consciousness, the phenomenalists do not exclude that from their endeavors to understand it. We should emphasize this point because it has an important theoretical marker. Functionalists conception of consciousness acknowledges its qualitative nature, thus admit to the central idea in the phenomenalists' conception. But, because they have no means to identifying that materialistically they deny its material existence. Dennett agrees "wholeheartedly" that there *seems* to be qualitative contents of mental states but he denies that they actually have material existence (1991).

The phenomenalists formalize a theory of what is experienced as consciousness. Their method is *inductive*; the main logical method in the human sciences. It approaches the observed subject and induces from it what would show its internal consistency, and derive its validity from that internal consistency. We find this way of thinking in good structural theories. Phenomenalists disputed the arguments of the functionalists but did not provide an answer to this question: if subjectivity, content, and the other qualitative aspects of consciousness are intrinsic attributes that go beyond the materialistic nature of the brain then where, how, and what creates them? The phenomenalists were seeking a match between the subject and his mind and leaving the match between the brain and the mind to the functionalists. But, it is not enough to change terminology to avoid making sense of consciousness. The search for the origin of consciousness is unavoidable.

THE PUZZLING IMPASSE

The two schools neither supported their merits totally nor disqualified the merits of the challenging school completely. As must be expected, something else had to come out of that situation. The advanced interest in consciousness and cognitive sciences took off after the demise of behaviourism in the fifties of the last century. The interest in *the mental* and not only *the behavioural* brought back the concept of *representation* to the field of psychology. This concept was an important concept in European psychology, as the work of Brentano (1929)—that was recently translated—has shown. The innovations in the field of instrumental investigations of neural activity provided unexpected knowledge about the brain and stimulated research in the neurological corollary of the psychical. Gradually, the two streams came to meet at the concept of *the mind*. It was not possible for the functionalists to continue denying the existence of something beyond the brain, as the phenomenalists had no grounds to stand on talking about mental activities that have no source in the organ of mental functions. Bit by bit, the questions arose in the literature about the setting where cognition materializes or sets off, and indirectly the possible additional sources for consciousness, beside the brain. Those questions were, point in fact, a new query about subjectivity in conscious experiences. The neurologists seemed to be capable of explaining most of consciousness in neurological terms, except subjectivity and its content. The phenomenalists were able to bring about the varied subjective contributions to consciousness, which needs to be addresses neurologically. In other words, the argument boiled down to the inability of the functionalists to give a neurological explanation of the "subjective" nature of conscious experience, and the phenomenalist incapable of accounting to the engendering of independent subjectivity that, nevertheless, becomes part of consciousness.

Somehow, reducing the problem to this singular issue enables examining a new section of work that both schools are using to advance their claims; the embodiment of consciousness or the incarnation of consciousness. The term *embodiment* "means that the concepts of the mind are crucially shaped by the body. Embodiment school claims that the properties of concepts are the outcome of the way the brain and body interact in interpersonal relations and in relating to the physical world (Lakoff and Johnson 1999). This new approach emerged to consider the whole phenomena of cognition and consciousness to be products of a compounded interaction of the body or the sensory-motor system, the nervous system, and the external world. Therefore, consciousness has become a manifestation of the human subject and not merely the mental aspect of individual existence. Consciousness is the whole body in addition to the external world generating what is termed the subject. The external world and the whole body together are sources and receivers of stimulation, that is, the body stimulates the brain and the brain stimulates the body and the product is the human subject.

Human consciousness is distinct compared to even the closest primates to our species. It is true that our consciousness is quantitatively more complex and advanced. It is also true that humans were able to turn the advancement of their ancestors' consciousness into more advancement, while the rest of the animal kingdom remained unchanged. Better, the human race is continuing the process of evolution, which is arrested in higher primates. Language, an early creation of the human mind, has and still is changing from a means to communicate to becoming an integral part of human thinking and culture. In this culture of information language is more a reservoir of knowledge than just a means to create it. But, the research in the nature of human consciousness remained fixed on the ontological and comparative conditions of its phenomena. Fixated on consciousness as an "event" keeps thinkers puzzled, and shifts the emphasis away from the way they think about it. This new approach acknowledges that *humans differ from the rest of the animal kingdom in the specific and multifaceted ways their brains and their bodies interact producing a human subject and not just a member of the human species.*

Before reaching this advanced point, cognition was considered a science of the rules and the laws that govern the perception and the awareness of the external world, and little attention was given to the human subject as the originator of his cognition. Cognition was disincarnated. With the rise of the issue of the mind, as the scene of cognition and the housing of consciousness, came a push toward re-incarnating it. But the brain was not enough to explain the mind because it has to contend with external stimuli, stimulation from the body, and its own neurological structures and functions, which it has to create and respond to at the same time. Wilson says (2002): ". . . the mind must be understood in the context of its relationship to a physical [brain] that interacts with the world. . . . Hence human cognition, rather than being centralized, abstract, and sharply distinct from peripheral input and output, may instead have deep roots in sensorimotor processing" (625).

The embodiment movement came with its set of problems. Wilson (2002) identifies a division between two main streams: the first puts the emphasis on embodied cognition of the immediate interaction with the external world, or the on-line interaction (situated cognition), cognition as a reaction to the immediate and active environment. Thus, there is no mental mediation between stimulation and response. The other stream emphasizes cognition of distant non-immediate stimulation, off-line interaction, where the external world helps in creating representations (mental mediators) that contribute to the mental manipulations of the environment. The work of Lakoff and Johnson (1980) shows that our thinking, which is our consciousness and cognition combined, is based on engendering of metaphors. They are mainly of the body, but also of the external world as it interacts with our body. The problem looks as if the division between the functionalists and the phenomenalists has changed, and a new division is now between two other schools: classical embodiments and radical embodiment (Reboul 2012). The first has room for mental activity, that is, representation as a step toward considering the emergence of the mind and the mediators of the online responses. The latter, has no place for a middle stage between input and output. Chemero explains that by saying: "In embodied cognitive science, some of the intelligence is 'off-loaded' from the brain to the body and environment" (2011, 27). The arguments in that school confuse brain's utilization of the bodily states and the bodily states dictating on the brain its limitations. Although there is debates between the two "camps" about coupling and decoupling representation and its source, those debates (to the extent I know of the literature) avoid, bypass, ignore the issue of causality. Is the emergence of the mind a function of the activities of the embodied brain (caused by the brain), or the link is not causal and those two matters are decoupled?

The main and, in fact, the only difference between those two schools is in the meaning and place of the concept of representation in the mental process. Chemero (2011) takes the extreme position that every representation is coupled to its object and is in causal relationship with it. Sometimes it is decoupled to perform its function in another system, and when its object has no place in that system. The most significant point in this radical stand is that representation is considered a product of the subject to match the external object, in that sense it has a causal relationship with it. Chemero says: "Because representations are posited as theoretical entities and because they do explanatory work in virtue of the information they carry, a theory of representation needs to explain how something [a representation] inside an agent could become something outside the agent . . ." (ibid. 50).

Representation, which took the place of subjectivity in the disputes between the functionalists and the phenomenalists *has to be examined in terms of a distinction between representing an external cognitive object, and representing an internal somatic pressure.* The former is something that may be subject to those kinds of discussions and arguments. External stimuli could be examined and submitted to the scrutiny of a third-party, because they are dealt with through respective sensory organs. The endosomatic stimuli have no distinctive organs to sort them out and subject them to the scrutiny of recognition. They are recognizable at a certain stage of exerting pressure on the mind but unidentifiable entities unless their representations are different.

THE PUZZLING LITERATURE

The arguments about consciousness were centered on *what*, *where*, and *how* the conscious experience happens. Those three adverbs are the core of the puzzle of consciousness because each depends on the other to get an answer. If there is a definite *how* then there would be a chance to know *what*. If we know *what* we could hope then to know *where* will it be found? But, since they are all three unknown entities (at least not definitive entities) they would probably get the thinkers into a muddle. Thinking about consciousness seems to be going in two opposite directions; the functionalists are going away from the specific problem of subjectivity, while the phenomenalists are going toward it, but both with no clear vision of what they are searching for. The functionalists believe (hope) that they will prove that subjectivity is a distraction from the main endeavor to define consciousness in the language of the third person; it has no place in the measurement and observation of its material source. The phenomenalists consider subjectivity the starting point in any profound investigation and definition of consciousness. It does not take much to realize from the wide-ranging literature that those two directions—in the most optimistic view—are going in circles and would never meet. The ambition that the embodiment of consciousness might bridge the gap between the first party's language of representations and the language of the third party's measurement disappear when we see how embodied cognitive theories comprise the process of representation itself. The question here is the same again: is it conscious or "experiencing consciousness" that is a puzzle.

The attempts at delineating the experience of being conscious led some thinkers (Blackmore 2005; Combs 2009) to specify three of its characteristics: continuity, content, and self-ness. A conscious experience comprises a sense of *continuousness*. Even if interrupted for any reason its interruption is experienced as dis-continuity. The experience of being conscious is an experience of something, that is, content. If a sense of content is absent there would be no consciousness. However, the absence of content could sometimes become the content of the experience; an experience of lack. The third characteristic is the sense of self-ness and of proprietorship. Experiencing a happening is never questioned as to who is experiencing it. Blackmore (2005) says: "whenever there are conscious experiences it is easy to assume they must be happening to someone; that they cannot be experienced without an experiencer" (67).

Those three attributes of conscious experiences should make us shift the emphasis from consciousness (the conscious) to *experiencing consciousness* (the experiencer). To wit, conscious experiences come to being only if there is an experiencer to experience them. Thus we should puzzle *first* about the subject of consciousness before or instead of puzzling about consciousness.

As there should be a thinker for thinking to transpire, there has to be a self for consciousness to be experienced. This is not a simple statement of incarnating a process, but a statement of emphasis of something lacking in the previous discussions. It is true that the perspective of the embodiment of consciousness presumes the presence of a subject, yet, it does not specify if the subject is a function of the process of consciousness or the originator of the process. Sperry (1975) was in the camp of the functionalist until he realized by his own research that brain activity does not account for the emergence of complex mental phenomena. He formulated a model where the mental affects the neural as the latter affects the former. He concluded *that the mind is an emergent product of such continuous interaction.* He says: "Conscious mental experience in our present interpretation is conceived to be a holistic emergent of brain activity, different from and more than the neural events of which it is composed, and a real phenomenon in its own right possessing causal potency in brain function" (ibid. 430). This sentence takes us back to Blackmore's depiction of the three attributes (mentioned above) that comprise experiencing consciousness. The holistic emergent phenomenon of brain activity is a reference to the experiencer, who is *his*-self. The "self" presents phenomenalists with questions of causality but not in a naïve functional way: Is the experiencer of consciousness the self? Is consciousness the experiencing of myself? The main idea is that the self is the amalgam of all the different types and degrees of experiencing consciousness. This leaves us speculating about the formation of the self out of that amalgamation, or maybe the way a sense of self could put all those experiences in one stable formation.

A main problem, which neither the functionalists nor the phenomenalist addressed is consciousness of consciousness (the transcendence of consciousness). Nonetheless, the main feature in the transcendence of consciousness is its duality: One can know and can also know that he does know. In other terms, human consciousness takes the self in itself as a subject of consciousness.[3] The transcendence of consciousness is behind some aspects of consciousness that does not have a prominent place in the literature: *what is the sense of self*? How do I come to know that *I* am *he* that is *me*? Knowing that one knows, feeling that one feels, knowing that one does not know or does not feel is a human attribute; not just because we do not see it in other animals, but because we humans differ widely in the manifestations of that attribute. Any attribute that represents individual differences *is* human, because animals may differ from other animals but they do not differ amongst themselves. There are bigger elephants and smaller elephants but they are all elephants, after all.

Most of the endeavors regarding consciousness were mainly centered on human consciousness, but were implicitly predisposed to comparisons with consciousness in animals. This implicit stance ignores two things: Human consciousness is distinct from consciousness in the rest of organic life, because its variations within our species are non-existent in the other species. It serves other functions than connecting us to the environment; it also connects us to each other. As mentioned before, all the neurological processes that result in cognitive experiences do not happen in consciousness, that is, *what creates consciousness is unconscious*. The process that creates consciousness of the self is unconscious to the self. The unconscious processes that are active behind consciousness seem to find ways and means to infiltrate consciousness and give it an individual shade (subjectivity). The obvious distinguishing aspect in human consciousness, which is overlooked, is the human subject is the experiencer of the experience. This should have been the starting point in debating the issue.

The second thing is that self-awareness, not cognition, is the true and most solid manifestations of human consciousness. All primates have similar nervous systems and sensory-motor systems similar to humans, but the only outcome of their activities is cognition. In humans, the activity of those systems brings *him* to being; his *him* would then do the cognition.

Velmans says (2009): ". . . theories of consciousness that do not in some way deal with its phenomenology are not theories of consciousness" (10). This indomitable statement is right if consciousness is merely an ontological issue, but because it also has a metaphysical meaning to some, it should be taken in proviso.

NOTES

1. Phenomenalism looks at the structure of the subject matter of a phenomenon. It concentrates on the manner the phenomenon has its characteristics and the way those characteristics are internally configured. Thus, it looks for links that when interpreted properly would reveal what could be studied objectively later (if possible).

2. Phenomenology was an early conception of structuralism as the antithesis of functionalism.

3. William James's distinction between the *I* and *Me* is very important, as we will explain further in chapter six. For now we could say that *Me* processes consciousness and *I* becomes conscious of it. Better, what processes consciousness is *Me* but *I* is who experiences it.

Chapter Two

The Two Approaches to the Enigma of Consciousness

Velmans, a phenomenalist, says (2009): "If one makes up one's mind about the ontology of phenomenal consciousness before fully investigating how its phenomenology relates to processing in the brain and the surrounding world, one precludes a deeper understanding of that ontology" (152). The issue as we saw from comparing the two approaches to consciousness is the futility of waiting for one of the two methodologies to solve the puzzle of consciousness on its own, and the uselessness of expecting the two schools to meet at a point of merger as long as the definition of consciousness is not agreed upon by both schools. The way Velmans put it has to be looked at differently: the ontology of consciousness is illusive because the objective of research is to find a way (or ways) to match two paralleled lines of thought and make them meet at the end. The phenomenalists' endeavor is know more about consciousness as means to understanding the mind, and indirectly the human subject. The functionalists' approach is to learn more about the brain to match its activities to the manifestations of consciousness, and eventually to have a scientific meaning of the self.

The phenomenalists seem to have no sense of problem with their methodology or with their terminology. From the looks of it, the phenomenalists can only improve their claim by revealing more aspects of consciousness that are difficult to explain neurologically. However, apart from Freud,[1] there is not much added by the phenomenalists' to the theory of consciousness. On the other hand, the functionalists have a problem with both their methodology and terminology. Damasio pointed out two main approaches in neurology regarding consciousness (2012). One approach is examining conscious processes as neuro-activities of the brain to reach and formulate a materialistic conception of the mind. This scientific conception of the mind we could have no place for speculating about the human subject. As we will see later, this methodology had to coin some non-neurological terminology to fit their methodology. The other approach starts from the characteristics of the human subject as a *self*. Those "fewer" neurologists argue that starting from the characteristic of the self would lead to understanding the neuro-activity of the brain and to a better conception of the mind. The two approaches within the functionalist camp make consciousness more of an enigma than a puzzle. They both know the brain equally well and share the same terminology, but adopt two opposite methodologies: one deductive (from the details to the whole) one inductive (from the whole to the details). Therefore, I will present the two approaches through the work of Gerald Edelman and Giulio Tononi who believe that consciousness is explainable purely in materialistic terms, and Damasio who aspires to give the self a purely materialistic explanation.

In the last three decades neurosciences have taken big strides in investigating the anatomy, physiology biochemistry and the neural activity of the brain. There is no question that those investigations have widened and deepened the understanding of neuro-activities in profound and unprecedented ways. Notwithstanding, the questions about consciousness are not answered satisfactorily yet. Reviewing the contemporary literature shows that neurologically there is very little more data needed to solve the puzzle of consciousness, yet something is still lurking in the background thwarting those attempts. For instance, Edelman and Tononi (2000) maintain that there is no substance of "consciousness" that is separate from brain substance. They expanded and enriched their repertoire of arguments, but the enigma still defies matching brain activities and some mental indicators of those activities. They are unable to explain how the neural activity in the Broca area makes us talk, while the activity in the Wernicke's area makes us understand what is said, although they are both made of the same neural substances.

FROM BRAIN TO SELF

Edelman and Tononi (2000), two staunch functionalists, lay down their position by saying: "consciousness is not an object but a process and that, looked at from that point of view, is indeed a fitting scientific subject" (ibid. 9). They identify, in this statement, their logic of approaching consciousness: it is not something to study but a process that engenders it in the subject of the study. The method of studying that process is stated as "scientific." They specify three methodological assumptions about consciousness: consciousness is a physical process, granted that it is a special one,[2] it has features that are explicitly human and not shared by other animals, and its qualitative nature tallies known complex structural changes in the human brain. They conclude that if those characteristics are explainable physically we can then rely on purely scientific descriptions of consciousness.

The two authors prescribe few points that follow from their methodological analysis of consciousness. One of them in particular deserves more attention. They noted that humans do things and comprehend what they did *after* the doing. If that is the case, then humans must have two consciousnesses: one that is needed for doing followed by another which comprehends the first one,[3] that is, consciousness of consciousness. They admit that this is a problem, but they put it in neurological terms by saying: "Why should the activity of certain nerve cells, or neurons, in the brain correlate with the succession of private (subjective) phenomenal states that we call conscious experience, while that of other neurons is deprived of such remarkable property" (ibid. 17). They relate that to the assumption that some *locality* in the brain does the acting and another does the comprehending with a continuous feedback between them; they call the feedback reentry.[4] This neurological explanation is not substantiated independently (scientifically), but *proposed* as a working hypothesis. The reentry explanation stands against what their attestation that: "each conscious state is experienced as a whole that cannot be divided into independent components" (ibid. 18). Because the brain functions as a whole, presumably with no gap between acting and conceiving the act, they needed another assumption to support the notion of reentry; *they assumed the existence of a dynamic core for neural activities.*

The two authors go on to reveal more evidence that neurological activities explain conscious aspects, yet the sum of those aspects is always less than the totality of the phenomenon. Their concept of reentry supposedly takes care of that discrepancy. Conscious experiences could generate without external input (off-line), which means that consciousness could be a response to purely internal stimulation (an issue we will get to in chapter five). However, neurological disorders affect consciousness in manners that defy this straightforward description. When there are anatomical divisions in the brain due to dysfunctions or surgical intervention the ensuing gaps in conscious experiences are covered up falsely by quasi-conscious material. This phenomenon and several others (sited by the two authors) suggest a deficiency of a true *material* correlation between consciousness material and neural activity material.

They ask a question and use their answer to respond to the peculiarities of neuropathology: *why should the simple differentiation between light and dark performed by a human being be associated with consciousness experience, while that performed by photodiode is not*? The answer, as they say, is that a human being selects from a repertoire of possible responses, while the photodiode does not have that facility in its structure. The reply to that is: the human being, despite his limitless repertoire of experiences, needs only the experience of dark and light to respond in that example. Nevertheless, he still responds to light and darkness with rich conscious feelings that darkness and light engender in him. Even if we connect the device to a computer with the repertoire of experiences the human has, it will still respond without the experience of consciousness.

Edelman and Tononi (2000) give a clear and thorough exposition of the brain and its neurological functions. They talk about its "architecture" and its function and come up with a wide range of description of its activity. I will try to underline the main features they find useful in explaining the neurological foundation of consciousness. The *first* feature is the complexity of the brain's anatomical structure and the efficacy and sufficiency of that structure to be the base for consciousness as a process along with it as an entity. The structure of the brain connects all its parts and localizations in one functional network. The *second* feature is the existence of regions in the brain that have specific functions, like Wernicke's area for language comprehension and Broca's area for language production, but those regions are interconnected in a way that could activate any combination of them at a specific moment. Consciousness is a product of the integration of most of the brain regions and its internal connections relates directly or indirectly to that conscious experience. The *third* feature is the continuous rapid reentrant interactions between the regions of the brain, thus initiating integrated and differentiated patterns of activities that are interrelated to consciousness.

The phenomenalists' claim that the presumed cause-effect relationship between consciousness and brain activity is not yet based on solid evidence, thus they feel justified in rejecting the functionalists' argument. They are right in another way. The functionalists' argument is based on a subtle twist of logic.[5] By reversing the cause effect link Edelman and Tononi put the matter this way: the complexity of conscious experience entails corresponding complex brain activity. They use the complicated model of brain functions to support the validity of proposing a dynamic neural core behind all mental phenomena to explain the complexity of consciousness. In other words, instead of actually finding in the brain the material evidence of the complexity of consciousness, they used the complexity of consciousness to propose a brain structure that could explain such complexity. They say: "the activity of a group of neurons can contribute directly to conscious experience *if* (my emphasis) it is part of a functional cluster; characterized by strong mutual interactions among a set of neural groups over a period of hundreds of milliseconds" (ibid. 139). The suggested dynamic core is a hypothesis and cannot be used—as a cause—to prove anything before it has been proven first.

This logical lapse led them to another one about *representationality*; the anathema of functionalism. They defined memory "as the ability of a dynamic system that is molded by selection and exhibits degeneracy to repeat or suppress a mental or physical act" (ibid. 93). They meant that a neurophysiological explanation of memory implies that it is not a reservoir of some sort of content, and it is only a system of selecting the recall of mental or physical acts. They use that hypothetical formulation of memory to pounce on the concept of representationality—a central concept in the phenomenalists' school. Since the prevailing conception of memory infers a reservoir of representations, therefore they reasoned that neural activity has no place for representationality. Yet, to support this new assumption they resorted to a metaphor (representational par-excellence) that memory is like a glacier that melts and refreezes not as writing on stone. It is interesting they do not specify who writes on the stone or keeps rewriting on the glacier.

They admit—at the end—that the information in the content of a state of consciousness has to do with the emergence of a conscious *state of self*, which is instrumental in making consciousness a personal and subjective experience. Moreover, they stipulate that consciousness is awareness of being situated in time and space; consciousness is a state of sentience and being. Even if the stimulation is external, consciousness of the external still does not have to be related to the external world (ibid. 32–33). Those two metaphysical issues (let alone their ontological significance) obliged the authors to address the problem of *qualia,* because of its centrality in self-reference and subjectivity. Their approach to the issue of qualia exposed another erroneous logical stance. They summarize their view about qualia by maintaining that:

1. *Quale has to be a product of a brain in a body*; which is a sensible but not a determining factor.
2. *Each different conscious experience is a separate quale, which corresponds to a different state of the dynamic core (discussed above)*. This extrapolation was explained by the third postulate.
3. Each *quale corresponds to a different dynamic core, which is the expression of differentiated neural groups that comprise billions of integrating neurons*. In addition to the absence of any new evidence to that statement it is based on begging its own question: how do we have the potential for unlimited qualia experiences.
4. Finally they resort to explaining *those potential as rooted in the embryonic autonomic and kinesthetic endowment of the person*.

The fourth postulate leads us to a leap in logic: we are endowed with the potential to have quality to our consciousness, thus the neurophysiological activity explanations describe consciousness, which is explainable by neurophysiological endowment; a little different from the phenomenalists' but as ineffective.

The functional approach had to address an unexpected problem related to deductive logic: if consciousness is a product of brain activity then brain activities should have a place in consciousness. However, not all neurophysiological activities result or manifest in mental or physical displays. Neuropsychological studies showed that a great part of cognitive activities are non-conscious, that is, they do not translate into observable phenomena in spite of their requisite participation in cognition. All the activities in the brain are un-conscious, even the ones assigned by the functionalists as the *cause* of consciousness. Therefore, the cause-effect relationship between the brain and consciousness had to be restated, so that the non-conscious neural activities would be accounted for.[6]

Addressing that problem, the functionalists *resorted* to dividing consciousness into different dualities: unconscious-conscious, primary consciousness-high order consciousness, and mental life I and mental life II. Primary consciousness, which we share with other animals that have a nervous system controlled by a brain, is the basis of the fixed and autonomous cognitive and behavioral responses; for example, the instinctual and non-thinking responses. The high-order consciousness is specifically human because it accounts for the features of abstract thinking and the entwinement of thought, symbolic categorization of external stimuli, linguistic mentation, and quale, which activate each other.

The conception of primary consciousness (mental life I, unconscious) required specifying its difference in phenomenal terms. I quote Edelman and Tononi (2000) saying; "Unconscious aspects of mental activities, such as motor and cognitive routines, and so-called unconscious memories, intentions, and expectations play a fundamental role in shaping and directing our conscious experiences. . . . Such unconscious routines, which are both motor and cognitive, involve long, parallel neural loops running through cortical appendages such as the basal ganglia and the cerebellum" (121). This quotation shows that the unconscious or primary consciousness has a phenomenal content, but the neurological localization of its loops does not answer to the causation of its content. The same we find in defining the high-order consciousness. The authors state that high-order consciousness is the outcome of some neural changes that allow language to emerge! The formation of the high-order consciousness results in the emergence of a sense of self (consciousness of consciousness!). As they say: "The emergence of the self leads to the refinement of phenomenological experience, tying feelings to thought, to culture, and to beliefs" (ibid. 193). The "desperate" attempts at a functional explanation of consciousness end up being no more than efforts to construct a neurological model that matches the phenomenological attributes of consciousness, with only physical and concrete evidence of neural activities that accompany those hypothetical reentry neural passages, the dynamic core and a neurological distinction between mental life I and II. The evidence is either anatomical, or morphological, but not of the same *material*.

Detecting the logical (methodological) flaws in the functional approach to consciousness does not preclude Edelman and Tononi's (2000) logical deduction that: "consciousness is a physical process embodied in each unique individual, and that embodiment can never be substituted for by a mere description" (ibid. 207). The functional approach of the type Edelman and Tononi represent could be founded on a concept of consciousness that is not appropriate for their methodology, thus compounding the problem. They derive their conception of consciousness from brain activities that are presumed existing in every (human) brain, thus should produce the same consciousness in all humans. This is the case in higher primates, but humans who have the same brains get different consciousnesses from it. Correcting the concept does not automatically correct the approach because working from the brain toward the mind will come to the gap between the signs of consciousness (neural activity) and its meaning (representation). This gap is unsurpassable from that direction; from the measurable to the immeasurable. It is similar to the gap found between the inorganic material and the organic material.

Could the functionalists reverse the direction and start from the immeasurable and material-less to the measurable and materialistic; from self to consciousness and the brain? Could the neurologist start from the differential attributes of human consciousness to end at the brain or the whole nervous system in humans?

FROM SELF TO BRAIN

A. Damasio made a "valiant" attempt at that and very skillfully; strangely without much success until now. He expresses this idea (2010) by saying: "The neuroscience of consciousness is often approached from the mind component rather than the self" (194). The reason is maintaining the same deductive thinking of the extreme functionalists, which forces the thinker to confine his research to matching two entities—that are qualitatively different—in order to discover a cause-effect link between them.[7]

Damasio specified two problems with studies in consciousness in general. The first is explaining how the brain genders images of the external objects (mental representations). Related to that problem is the problem of qualia; although he believes that it will eventually find a neurological solution. The second problem is the mirror image of the first one: how the brain gives birth to a sense of self (self-representation). Related to the complexity of mental representations of the external world is the inevitable linkage of object representation to self-representation, for example, the mental representation of the external world is, for all means and purposes, *my* making (subjectivity). The novelty in Damasio's approach, despite its heavy neurological "flavor," is approaching consciousness not from its inception in the brain, like all neurologists do, or from its end-result like phenomenalists do, but from a middle point: where a facet of consciousness presents simultaneously both the neurological and the phenomenal "thing." This approach is clearly expressed by Damasio in saying (1999): "Although I do not see consciousness as the pinnacle of biological evolution, I see it as a turning point in the long history of life" (4). This is a very important statement because it explains his different methodological stand.

He bases his theory on two main postulates (2004): The first is that most of the brain activity is not conscious; even some of its activity is not neural but chemically and endocrinologically generated. The other postulate is that emotions are a significant starting point in encompassing the phenomena of consciousness in an integrated theoretical framework. The notion that most of the activities in the brain are non-conscious is preserved in almost all the neurological, psychological, and cognitive science theories. It is not a new idea, but Damasio makes it a springboard to further elaborations. He considers those "unconscious"[8] neural activities the source of emotions. Emotions in his definition (which is different from the regular meaning it has in psychology and more like Freud's concept of affect) are unlearned sets of chemical and neural patterns, which arise when there are changes in the organism. The changes are mainly homeostatic or related to the survival of that organism. "Homeostasis is the coordinated and largely automated physiological reactions required to maintain steady internal states in the living organism" (Damasio, 1999, 39). In other words, Damasio starts his exploration of consciousness from the point of view that consciousness is a manifest of striving for life in the organism, which is the endowment of a set of chemical and neurological patterns that correspond to his survival and wellbeing needs (1999). He named the constitutional basis of life emotions, which, when triggered by a change in the organism's homeostasis, ensue after a chain of reactions.

Emotions are competent sets of responding to internal and external stimuli, matching between the external and internal stimuli, and can also produce stimulation that would contribute to the balance of the homeostasis. Damasio says the (1999): "emotions are part of the homeostatic regulation and are poised to avoid the loss of integrity that is a harbinger of death or death itself" (45). He identifies emotions in that elementary sense as an expression of the propensity for life saying: "[the] unconscious urge to stay alive betrays itself inside the simple cell in a complicated operation that requires 'sensing' the state of the chemical profile inside the boundary, and that requires unwitting 'unconscious knowledge' of what to do chemically speaking, when sensing reveals too little or too much of some ingredient at some place or time within the cell" (ibid. 138). Sensing in that model antecedes emotions in the complex organic forms.

He incorporates pain and pleasure in emotions as a vital evolutionary aspect of biological regulations in higher forms of life. He extends his point to introduce feelings as another level of the inherited sensory patterns which changes emotions into thoughts and images. He adds a significant note about emotions and its qualitative duality of pleasure/pain, and underlines the ability of certain chemicals to block pain without affecting pleasure or to enhance pleasure without blocking pain. He concludes that emotions are not simple reaction but comprises sophisticated measures of expressing pleasure and pain. Because emotions are responsible for the distinction between feelings of pain/pleasure Damasio makes another distinction between emotions and feeling, which he extrapolates to a distinction between emotions and brain activity on one side and feelings and mind on the other. He avers that emotions and brain activity are public and could be judged by third-party methods, while mind and feelings are private matters and personal.

Emotions attach to external and internal objects, therefore they establish links that get differentiated and distinguished from each other with experiencing those objects. Yet, they have the capacity—in a feedback loop—to affect the emotions that each other involve, thus create what he called *body-minded brain*; a brain that could prompt changes in the body. This new addition to the theory of emotive responses makes him consider emotions in a different way. He stipulates that although they are unlearned patterned sets of reactions and are inherently competent producing stimuli they show that they have the facility to return to their source and change it. So, they are not fixed sets but rather more of potentialities than modalities. This is how consciousness is borne.

The point about the body-minded brain leads him to the qualitative difference in human consciousness. The complexity of the human subject that includes his especial brain and its activity required two contributions from evolution: one anatomical and the other functional. The anatomical one is connecting the brain structures that manage the different aspects of human life to a neural system that is multi-sectioned; has multi areas that integrate those aspects in the same brain. The functional one is providing those regions with instantaneous information about the biological states of the person. This information is wrapped in the representations of the body (a central concept in his definition of consciousness but poorly defined), like the linguistic expression of bodily sensations and the sense of *self*.

Damasio talks about three types of self: 1. Proto-self which is totally unconscious because it represents the organic state of the human and is created by the multiple but mainly lower levels of the brain. 2. Core self which we are aware of though it is nonverbal. It comes to action when an object changes the proto-self. 3. The autobiographical self, which is us, the one we are conscious of. Although the three different aspect of *self* are epigenetically related they are products of different neural activities.

He defined five of the main "components" of the proto-self that are found to be functionally overlapping: 1. regulating the homeostasis; 2. participating in generating emotions and feelings; 3. attention; 4. wakefulness and sleep; 5. learning processes (1999, 273). Those components are fundamental in establishing the process of consciousness although they are not themselves conscious. Damasio, and neurologists in general, get confused by the fact that a major part of what they consider brain activity thus qualified to be sort of consciousness happens unconsciously. They suggested distinguishing between pairs of consciousnesses: primary and high-order consciousness, biological and psychological, sensory and noetic, conscious and unconscious. They could not find a probable link between those pairs of phenomena. Edelman and Tononi (2000) said: "it is likely that among the earliest conscious dimensions and discriminations are those connected with the body itself—mediated in the brain through structures in the brain stem that map the state of the body and its relation to both the inside and outside environment on the basis of multimodal signals that include proprioceptive, kinesthetic, somatosensory, and autonomic components (174). This is also Damasio's view of a primary consciousness controlled by the brain stem. Damasio built a model of the hierarchical organization of neural activity that leads in a natural way to consciousness. It is a theoretical framework and not an explanatory system.

In that framework the body is the foundation of the conscious brain; the homeostasis is the originator of the conscious brain. This view is different in essence from the notion of the embodiment of the brain, because Damasio does not see the body and the brain as two entities in unison. He treats the body almost like the cell in the unicellular organism, which has its consciousness within its structure without needing a separate nervous system. It senses the chemical changes in and around itself. Therefore, those primitive organisms have a homeostatic system that is one with its body. When the homeostasis begins to lose its balance in the human a *primordial feeling* arises. A primordial feeling is mapped in the brain as a natural reaction to homeostatic change, "*the primordial feeling precedes all other feelings. . . .*" (2010, 203).

Primordial feelings are the simple reactions of the body to homeostatic balances and imbalances and are either pleasure or pain. "One cannot fully explain subjectivity without knowing about the origins of feeling and acknowledging the existence of *primordial feeling . . . primordial feelings are the primitives for all other feelings*" (ibid. 108).[9] The parts of the body that are affected by the homeostatic changes are represented in the brain in the form of maps. They become the mental images of the body and constitute a *proto-self*. Those parts bombard the brain and get bombarded in a neural loop (ibid. 22).

The Damasio model could be recapped in these points:

- The self as object is a dynamic collection of integrated neural processes, centered on the representation[10] of the living body that finds expression in a dynamic collection of integrated mental processes.
- Consciousness is an organization of mind contents that are centered on the organism that produces those contents.
- The brain needs to acquire subjectivity to become conscious.
- Subjectivity is the feeling that what we experience is ours.
- When the brain manages to introduce *a knower* to the mind, subjectivity follows.

The main classical functionalists methodology lacks understanding that matching consciousness and neural activities does not add anything new to what is implicitly and explicitly known about consciousness; it will not bridge the gap between those two "events." The phenomenalists are not in a better position because they could only suggest more possibilities of the ontology of consciousness. Damasio's model has a salient advantage: *it attempts to match the self to consciousness through a neurological link.* Neurology is considered the scene where those two events get differentiated. He starts from a logical point: consciousness has to be initiated therefore it is an integral part of the living organism; the human subject. The body is the source of that initiation and its function (to preserve life) is represented in the brain in the form of maps (neural maps). They constitute a proto-self. Proto-self is the parts of the body that bombard the brain when they experience physical change and in a neural loop they get bombarded in return. Proto-self produces primordial feelings that originate in the brain stem and are degrees of pleasure and pain (ibid. 23). The objects that engage the feelings of the proto-self become part of the body image and modify the proto-self. In an intuitive remark about the link between the external world and the body image he says: "the representation of the world external can come into the brain only via the body" (ibid. 97). This is a basic conception of consciousness in the theory of the aconscious; representations come to us as perceptions of external sources and not as effects of the body.

Mapping is activated in a natural way when the subject interacts with the objects of his homeostatic imbalances. Consciousness (in Damasio's opinion) allows maps to become images, which is the material for reasoning. Images are mental patterns, which stem from neural patterns that stem from neural maps. The transformation of the initial mapping response into mental patterns (not only visual patterns but to any other sensory patterns like voice, etc.) changes the nature of the processes in an atypical way. Mapping as a neural activity could be monitored by a third party. Images on the other hand are private and not available to a third party's scrutiny. However, Damasio proceeds to say: "[they] are . . . logically interrelated, certainly when they correspond to events in the external world or in the body, which are, in and of themselves, governed by laws of physics and biology that define what we regard as logical" (ibid. 75).

The unfolding of the modified proto-self maps constitute a core self. The core self was preceded by the proto-self and together they become *me*. *Me* acquires a conscious mind resulting from several brain sites that integrate in one conscious event. The conscious mind emerges from the dynamics of the homeostasis, but it also recognizes a social homeostasis that operates as guardian of biological value (parenting). The conscious mind of *me* becomes aware of being surrounded by other selves; autobiographical selves that could monitor him and give him an autobiography of his own. The autobiographical self comes last and produces the social me or the *I*.

The body communicates hormonally and neurologically with the brain but, that is after the brain stem is activated. The basic elements of consciousness, like pain and pleasure starts in the mid brain. Communication is quantitative but it gets arranged in the mid brain because it has some permanent versions of its images. When it leaves the mid brain it gets organized in the cortices, and that is the qualia. The mind starts in the cerebral hemispheres. More and different events happen in the cerebral cortexes that are neither conscious dependent nor cognitive in nature. The brain "can *simulate*, within the somatosensory regions, certain body states, *as if* they were occurring; and because our perception of any body state is rooted in the body maps of the somatosensory regions, we perceive the body state as actually occurring even if it is not" (ibid. 109). This is a depiction of the phenomenon of fantasy which is a poorly defined psychical phenomenon.

Damasio uses his model to describe another psychical phenomenon which is known as *identification*. He says: "the brain's representation of the body has another major implication: because we can depict our own body states, we can more easily simulate the equivalent of body states of others. Subsequently, the connection we have established between our own body states and the significance they have acquired for us can be transferred to the simulated body states of others, at which point we can attribute a comparable significance to the simulation" (ibid. 111–112). Damasio built a perfect neuropsychological protocol that put brain and mind in the context of a human subject that is not yet finished evolving; therefore his consciousness is a puzzle. Nonetheless, the protocol as it is sketched is lacking a good understanding of the aconsciousness in the move from the homeostasis to the autobiography of the self.

In conclusion, the brain constructs consciousness by generating a self-process within an awake mind. The self is built of images that originate in the region that creates the proto-self (primordial feeling about the living body and the region of the object to be known). The multiple orders previously recorded form the biographical self. However, there is a feeling deeper than all of those mentioned, which is an enigma in its own right: *that my body exists, and it is present, independent of any object with which it interacts, as the rock-solid, wordless affirmation that I am alive, and that my mind belongs to me.* Yet we should not forget that the self is present in our minds in various and different degrees of clarity. We sense our selves differently at different circumstances. We differ in our sense of self too. Some sense their self in richly details and as a fully situated portrayal of who we are, while others sense it ever-so-faintly.

Damasio's model, despite its neurological base, is different. It is still deductive and functionally oriented but matching mind and self (successfully) makes it less far from the main point that both the purely functional and phenomenal are missing. The problem seems to me to be partially with Damasio's terminology because when I use the proper psychological and psychoanalytical terminology instead of his I find myself very close to a theory of consciousness. He created a whole lexicon to express his views, which is expected in a novel theoretical formulation but only if it is a terminology derived from the novel discovery.

NOTES

1. The last chapters of this book will deal with Freud's contribution to the theory of consciousness through his theory of the aconscious, which had a heavy neurological foundation.
2. What (Edelman &Tononi, 2000) they are proposing is ontologically and metaphysically problematic. They opted to bypass the problem of stating what are the differences in the neural activities of the brains of humans and primates, and if the brains we have are biologically and physiologically better, or just structural differently (15).
3. Later they introduce two designations to those consciousnesses: primary and high-order consciousness; and mental life I and mental life II.
4. Something of that nature was suggested by Freud (chapter four) but in a different context.
5. Reversing cause-effect relationships, especially when the link between the cause and its effect is not straightforward (broken), is a very tricky twist of logic. The functionalists say that since there is consciousness therefore there must be cause for its existence which is the brain. But, the complexity of consciousness made the functionalists make conscious complexities the *cause* and the complexity of the brain the *effect*. Subtly, the link remains the same though reversed to an undiscerning eye.
6. Lakoff & Johnson (1980, 71) say, "The concept of causation is often taken as an ultimate building block and undecomposed. Through their recurrence in our everyday functioning, the category of causation emerges with complex properties characterizing prototypical causation. When there is insufficient family resemblance to the prototype, we cease to characterize what happens as causation."
7. In chapter four I am presenting Freud's *Project of a Psychology for the Neurologists* , begun in 1895. It has an uncanny resemblance to Damasio's project of 'neurology for the psychologist'. The difference between the two projects is even more uncanny.
8. I am oscillating between the two terms; unconscious and non-conscious because as they are used by the functionalists and the phenomenalists they are different from the concept in the theory of psychoanalysis. In the familiar theory of psychoanalysis the unconscious is repressed conscious material. However, as I will explain in chapter six, psychoanalysis has another concept of the unconscious of psychical material that has no means to become conscious

although it is not repressed. I give that unconscious the term aconscious, like in amorphous, agnostic, asexual.

9. Subjectivity is a core content in the transcendence of consciousness. If it is a product of the primordial feeling of pleasure and pain we are thus required to understand the link between the subject as an object as-is, because there is an inherent aspect of "judgment" in that link too.

10. He defines representation as a "pattern that is consistently related to something," whether with respect to a mental image or to a coherent set of neural activities within a specific brain region (ibid. 320).

Chapter Three

Methodology, Terminology, and Missed Point

Terminology relates the words the speaker is using to the thoughts he is expressing. Therefore, it is very important for a speaker to clarify the meaning of what he says if he sees that others could be using (or understanding) his words differently. There is always an organic relation between thinking and the vocabulary used to express thoughts. Underlining that relation is important because words are not always precise while thoughts are supposed to be. Thus, a speaker should be held accountable for what he says after he clarifies what he means. The terms used by thinkers and researchers in the field of consciousness are, most of the time confusing, because they are given their meaning idiosyncratically without previous clarification. I will specify the meaning of some terms I will use to avoid mistaking the meaning I am giving them.

I am using awareness for unintended attention and non-deliberate consciousness, while I use consciousness for awareness that leads to intentional attention and purposive handling of its content. I am using brain to denote an organ of the nervous system and mind to mean the mental outcome of the embodiment of the brain. I am using "subject" to refer to the human unit in its abstract meaning, person for the human in his psychological sense, and individual for the subject in his social capacity. I am using the term methodology to identify the system of thinking used by the conflicting schools in the field. As is the case, neurologists researching consciousness (originally a psychological topic) are using terminology from psychological theories, but with different connotations that refer to neurology.

MATCHING NON-ANTITHETICAL ENTITIES

Bertrand Russell's puzzlement about qualia emerging from merely neural activity reveals an elementary reason why that could not and still is not resolved. The transformation from the quantitative to the qualitative state of anything is explainable if the subject matter of that change remains the same. Explaining the transformation of water into solid (ice) or gas (vapor) by changing its temperature is doable. But, explaining the transformation of neural pulsations, which are quantitatively measurable, into a mental or a psychological entity is not possible. It is not feasible to explain something that during the process of its transformation transmutes into something radically different. For instance, because the silk worm changes into a moth within a cocoon it weaves we are able to understand its transmutation. Logically, quantitative neurological changes are not what is behind qualitative consciousness. Looking more attentively or longer to a natural view does not lead to appreciating its beauty (quale). Increasing the intensity of the neural activity, in that example, could result in perceptual disturbances or neurological overload. Psychological research demonstrates that material gaps between the *percepts* and their *concepts* happen without the participation of consciousness in creating those gaps, for example, perception of an article of art and conceiving its beauty happen simultaneously and unconsciously.

The terminology used in those studies, like feedback, dynamic core, bilateral or reciprocal connections, global work place, etc., is terminology that fits a certain model of thinking. It is the *deductive* model of deriving from the configuration of the details the principle of their organization; a principle that requires naming. In deductive thinking, neural activities become a *neural dynamic core* that integrates them in a complex activity, which could seem more than the totality of their input. However, explaining the neural dynamic core does not lead to explaining qualia; it cannot—by itself—be the cause of such result. The problem is that qualia are not the antithesis of quanta; the increase in the quanta of neural activity could result in brain dysfunction, while the qualia of consciousness could emerge from the faintest of neural activity. They are opposites but not antitheses. Therefore, *matching* brain activity to conscious activity misses the point: they are not comparable activities to attempt matching them. Although there are reasons to consider a link between them it is not a functional link, because the initiator of each is not the same or even similar, and each has its course parallel to the other.

The phenomenalists are doing a similar exercise in matching two atypically related entities: the manifestations of consciousness and consciousness "in itself." Their effort of defining consciousness as a phenomenon makes them examine it as an *experience*. They need first to see it in a manner that would allow describing it. However, a question immediately arises: is that "experience" an experience of awareness, of awakeness, of knowing, of sense of self, etc.? They do not have a clear answer to those questions because they refer to intrinsic features of consciousness which allows few more to be added, without reservations. Another question regarding the conscious experience of the body arises here: do we perceive only the sensations that are coming from the body like feelings, thoughts, and states of mind, or do we also conceive of them as concepts like comfort, exhilaration, and contentment?

The phenomenalists strove to induce abstract understandings or meanings from conscious experiences that could match those experiences, whatever the subject matter of the experiences. They use *inductive* thinking as the method of approaching consciousness. The phenomenalist tries to put the details of varied conscious experiences under the abstract phenomenon of contentless consciousness. Nevertheless, conscious experiences are unique in nature; even when they are the private experience of the same person. They are to a great extent shaped by their content too. Thus, matching varied and concrete conscious experiences to one abstract condition is destined to failure. Phenomenal consciousness and the neural activity of consciousness are two terms reflecting predetermined adopted methods of thinking, and ultimately rejecting differing methods of thinking. Phenomenalists look at the aspects of the phenomenon only if their underlying structural configuration could be induced from their display. Presuming that consciousness is not understood and that there is more of it to know is problematic, because of the dormant disagreements on the aspect of the phenomenon of consciousness that could be inductively worked on.

Both schools focused on how to study consciousness, or what to study about it. They both missed that human brains seem to be tailored for each individual, or that individual consciousnesses mirror personal and not general brain activities. Missing this point made consciousness a puzzle to the majority of thinkers in the field. In addition to the inseparable bond between consciousness and its content, which is very particularized, there is a personal choice in constructing the conscious experience. It also remained an enigma for the functionalists' camp because in any approach they took to tackle the problem they ended up facing that puzzle. If they start from the brain toward the mind they come to face the individual's specific consciousness or *his-self*. The self needs to be bridged to get to the mind. If they start from the self in the reach for the mind, they still have to bridge it to match the brain. They end up meeting at the same point; the gap in matching two unmatchable entities.

This state of affairs should make us reiterate: is consciousness the problem or is the problem the experience of consciousness by the individual? If consciousness is not a product of "the brain" but of "an individual's brain," where do we go from there?

Missing this point is a result (in my opinion) of two things: the early interest in comparing human cognitive functions with those of the rest of the higher primates. The second is putting those comparisons in the context of the Darwinian theory of evolution. The difference between human consciousness and consciousness in other primates was referred, generally speaking, to anatomical and structural recognizable discrepancies between *us* and *them*. The structural aspects in the brain that gave humans the language capability, abstract manipulation of the environment, abstract thinking, the qualitative nature of perceptions, etc., engendered a different type of conscious experiences in humans. It made sense to concentrate on the nature and the specifics characteristics of *human consciousness* to learn something about the possible material differences between human brains and brains in higher primates. Better, since the anatomical and neurological differences between humans and higher primates were not major enough to notice therefore, research should identify the differences in the sphere of consciousness to guide us in discovering the unobvious material difference.

It was natural, thus, to distinguish between *awareness* and *consciousness* because awareness is a common phenomenon in all organic life; it is actually the signifier of living. We share that with all animal life. Members of any animal species share the same type of awareness, and differ from another species in the nature, type, and degree of awareness due to their particular anatomical and physiological endowments. In spite of those differences awareness in any species is not different in its efficacy in dealing with their particular environment. Their offspring are born with the same awareness, which, if needing time to mature, will become a replica of the rest of its species. Although comparing awareness among the whole animal kingdom shows the role of evolution in changing, and, to some extent, widening the scope of awareness in the more developed animals, awareness remained the same in each species since its origination. Awareness in animals, including higher primates, is one and the same, and its change from birth to maturity is minimal and basically predictable. It is feasible, even sensible, to look for functional links between the brain and consciousness in any animal species, except the human species.

Awareness in humans is fundamentally different. In humans our awareness always comes as consciousness.[1] *No two human brains are the same and no two human consciousnesses are similar.*

FUNDAMENTAL DIFFERENCES BETWEEN HUMANS AND OTHER PRIMATES

The very rudimentary feature of excitability in the protoplasm is the marker that differentiates between organic and inorganic matter. Responsiveness to change is the indication of life in a unicellular organism whether the change is external or internal. It is a precursor of consciousness. The excitability of all organisms in response to the environment, and the capability of changing it are indicative of an innate ability to respond. The need to respond is the originator of what evolves into awareness in multicellular organisms. This fact constitutes a substantial task ahead of the researchers in this field. They have to understand how the ostensibly simple responsiveness to stimulation evolved into awareness and eventually to consciousness in animals and further to consciousness of consciousness in humans.

The main endeavors to explain the emergence of life from inorganic matter is reiterated by Sheets-Johnstone (1998) quoting Paul M. Churchland saying that it happened "when near the surface of the ocean a purely chemical process produced 'some *self-replicating* molecular structures.'" The self-replicating molecular structure showed the additional capability of sensing changes in the balance of its internal and external environments. It revealed a sense of finality; a need to replicate to continue living. Although we do not have a solid explanation for the emergence of self-replication from mere sensitivity to change, we should consider it in our further investigation of consciousness. Sheets-Johnstone supports that idea with another quote from Daniel C. Dennett saying "in the beginning, there were no reasons: there were only causes. . . . There was nothing that had interest. But, after millennia, there happened to emerge simple *replicators*." She comments on that by saying: "Clearly, in both cases there is an attempt to separate out the inchoate creaturely from the 'purely chemical,' thus to specify the cosmic beginnings of life" (261). This view of the beginning of life is propositional but is sensible and a good start: a better start than the one offered by the creationists.

Dennett's distinction between cause and reason is very germane to the concept of transforming the simple chemical reaction that created life and produced replicators. A unicellular organic unit has a cause to stay alive, but has no means to remain living. In other terms; the amebae must have changed the cause for her living into a reason to replicate. Could awareness of death be what generated replication as a solution? By dividing and replicating the amebae continued living. Life impetus produced the reason for self-replication. The reason of self-replication was the onset of awareness: the discovery of the need to change. *Life is thus the originator of self-replication, and self-replication*[2] *is the originator of awareness leading to consciousness.*

It is a good start to examine consciousness from the point of view of the antithesis of cause and reason, because for evolution to happen a sort of dialectics is needed in that regard. Life and its antithesis of death created replication as the synthesis of both. Replication synthesises both life and death, but it also becomes a thesis in its own right. It sets up *difference* as its antithesis, which in turn engenders a synthesis that is different from the previous duality. The direct outcome of this dialectical model is a concept of evolution based on progression from lower to higher, from simple to complex and from the biological to the mental. There is a certain implied principle in that conception: evolution is quantitative changes that when they reach a certain point in evolving they turn into qualitative leaps (as some quantitative changes in the chemistry of some inorganic matter led to the qualitative change of becoming organic protoplasm). This is a useful principle and a valid one in physics and maybe in some aspects of the humanities too. However, when it comes to consciousness we should be cautious in applying it blindly.

All living organisms are equal in their adaptation to their environment, that is, their awareness is adequate for survival in the kind of environment they live in. Thus, our awareness, in principle, is not qualitatively better than the awareness of a worm, in terms of competence to survive. Also, awareness of the environment is not dependant on the existence of a nervous system. A jellyfish has no nervous system and is as efficient in surviving in the ocean as the best shark. The star fish with a very elementary central neural nodule coordinates the movement of its five limbs as well as it needs, and as effectively as a flying bird moves its wings.

We should also consider another reservation in accepting a simple quantitatively based concept of evolution (Denton, 1986). Evolution does not follow a linear course of development that points to its aim. The creation of multicellular organism and more complex structures did not end the creation of the unicellular organisms. Accordingly, evolution's aim is not to improve life, but to preserve it by continuing the process of diversity; otherwise, the latest of the advanced forms of life should have been the only existing results of evolution. Each creation continues to replicate and coexist with the newer evolved ones. If there is any reason for evolution it would be the unlimited number of chances for a dialectical dual to produce syntheses.

The advanced organic structures usually have new differentiated and specialized cells. Those cells could perform additional and different functions, and they ultimately form new organs for that function. The new complex organic entities are structured with *potential* for more functions. The advancements of organic structures, equipped with those new potentials, are able and have *reasons* to explore new environments and eventually use those newly formed organs to adapt to the those environments. The new environment requires modifications in awareness, which in turn requires changes in the structuring of the organic in order to unite to create new organs. Fish that tried living for moments out of the water (fishing for insects) developed a few specialized cells to absorb oxygen from the air and dissolve it in the blood stream. Some, after advancing this potential, became amphibious. They were able to survive out of the water and their awareness had to respond to the new environment. *Evolution builds new organic structures and their awareness obliges modifications in those structures.*

The simple quantitative Darwinian conception of evolution faces a major challenge in examining consciousness in humans. All species have their adequate sense of awareness. It could differ in complexities from one species to another, but they are all equal in their efficacy. Therefore, awareness in the animal kingdom—with exception of humans—is easy to study, define, and compare. Functionalism and phenomenalism are suitable methods at that level. Human consciousness is difficult to compare with other consciousness in the animal kingdom, because in addition to its qualitative differences there are major differences *within* the human race in consciousness; not all humans are equal in their conscious aptitudes. The differences within the human species in consciousness identify it as a unique feature of life in that species; it goes beyond the physical usefulness. Although we live and die like all organisms, between those two ends consciousness is not the same amongst all humans.

These arguments might look more like a succession of hypotheses, but it is also a methodical way of dealing with intrinsic problems within a simplistic conception of evolution. We need to address some questions that appear to be without an answer: is every elementary awareness a separate system in its own right? Is there a conscious process behind evolution? Is consciousness in organic matter what changes and guides the process of evolution? Does the creation of varied and advanced organic systems follow a sort of awareness of the process and the aim behind it, which is beyond our comprehension? I do not think we have answers to those questions but we have reasons for asking them.[3]

BASIC PROPERTIES OF HUMAN CONSCIOUSNESS

Human consciousness does not yield itself to comparisons with awareness in other animals. It is unique because it is not just an advanced point in the evolution of animal brain activities, but because, in its own right, it underwent and is still undergoing evolution and change. Human consciousness has properties that deserve especial attention.

Human consciousness has evolved in leaps and bounds since the emergence of the first homo-sapient, while other animals once they reached the limits of their awareness they stayed there. Three main features are recognizable as foundational for all further changes in human consciousness: communication (messaging and getting messages), manipulating the environment mentally (off-line mentation), selective sexuality (replicating for reason and by choice). Although the first homo-sapiens experimented with their new potentials, they continued experimenting, thus progressing; they continued improving those potentials. Humans benefited from each other; the young learned from the old but surpassed them and learned from the learned and improved on them. Their evolution was not solely physical. The rest of the animal kingdom did not transmit their potentials beyond what is already achieved by natural evolution. *Human consciousness is not confined to the physical limitation of the brain, because it is capable—in different degrees—to benefit from the brains of others.*

Human consciousness is also cumulative. For instance, in the last three centuries the human species discovered and gained knowledge far more than what was discovered and achieved in the previous ten thousand centuries. However, it was impossible to achieve that without the start in the Old Stone Age. Whatever human thinking reaches, and looks like an end, turns out to be the beginning of a new progress. This characteristic of human consciousness is not only inter-generational but it is also intra-psychical. Human consciousness benefits from itself. There are signs that humans in the last few decades are accelerating their evolution purposely, because every new discovery changes the sense of need to pursue it further in a way that suggests intuitions of what to come next. There are no indications that animals benefit from the awareness of their ancestors or other animals around them.

In the rest of the animal kingdom all members of the same species show the same *trends* of awareness regardless of age, gender, environment, or experience. A distinctive attribute of human consciousness is the vastness of the qualitative discrepancies amongst the individual members of that species. Those discrepancies play very obvious roles in differentiating between groups within the human race. This feature tells us that consciousness in humans is not a constitutional endowment; it is a constitutional prospective.

Human consciousness is coupled to the event of speech which is an improved way of messaging. Animals communicate concretely by sound and other direct means, but humans turned those inherited aspects into speech, which eventually became language. Whether the existence of specialized regions in the brain for language in homo-sapiens or their growing need for messaging initiated brain change is not the point. Turning the potentialities of speaking into language and using it had and still has an effect on human awareness. It turns it into consciousness and turning consciousness into thought.

We now come to an attribute of consciousness that is not only specific to humans but fundamental to any sensible approach we take to studying consciousness. In all animals there is nothing to call sick or abnormal about their awareness; they either have it or lose it for physical or material causes, and when they lose it the animal becomes simply dysfunctional and dies. There are no depressed giraffes or inhibited lions. Consciousness in humans is different because it gets affected by physical and non-physical reasons, and changes and stays changed without losing it. It changes to be considered abnormal and pathological. In some affected cases consciousness becomes only eccentric, but in others it is outright sick. Contrary to what happens in animals we could still live and perform despite the pathological conscious functions, which are deviations in different degrees from the "normal" conditions of consciousness. When consciousness is disordered the human subject manifests that disorder, while his physical and social identities remain unaffected. A healthy bright successful scientist could remain functional while being paranoid and dysfunctional in a particular area of his life. Changes that could affect the physical and social identity of a person pertain to his *psychological* makeup. Changed consciousness in a person changes him as a human subject.

In humans, selective replicating (sexuality) is not just for that cause; it is significant in many ways. I will concentrate only on one: sexuality in humans is separated from its biological cause or purpose. It is not triggered by vital or organic urges of copulating because it has become part of human consciousness, that is, deliberate attention. Humans select and choose their sexual mates; they turn replication into an act that extends beyond sexual intercourse. It involves choosing the mate and caring for the offspring with that sexual mate. It has become an act influenced by social and moral values, that is, it is no longer a blind urge to replicate but an act of more than one purpose. It is not easy to ignore the immense conscious involvement in the act of replications in humans with its unlimited psychological impact on consciousness, and the formation of the human subject. In addition to all of that, we still cannot ignore the change in the values of life and death in humans and, as part of consciousness, the act of replication. They all lose, almost completely, their unconscious meaning (their primordial origin) and become totally of psychical meaning in the human experience of consciousness.

EVOLUTION OF THE MIND IN HUMANS AND IN THE HUMAN SUBJECTS

The branching out of the homo-sapient species from the main branch of the primates was evidence of a major genetic mutation. The mutation was of several physical and biochemical changes that were to unravel gradually in a final reach of their full potentials. One of those genetic mutations was the gradual restructuring of the brain,[4] since the marvel of a brain dominating a nervous system was already accomplished in lower levels of genetic evolution. It took two million years for the homo-sapient brain to show its first qualitative changes of directed attention, few hundreds of thousands of years for those changes to produce the characteristics of consciousness, and only a few thousand years to cross the final chasm between us and our ancestors and enter the phase of early civility and civilization with the transformation of consciousness into thinking. What characterizes this leap is sudden and clear emergence of all what we consider the potentials of our modern mind. I will mention only four.

1. The trend and potentiality of communicating about none present matters and transmitting that communication between different individuals, in different timeframes. Humans started to message each other on the most primitive scale when they were planning their hunting and food gathering.

2. Turning mental products like ideas or feelings into visual or auditory equivalents. Transforming an idea into a specific sound or form allowed messaging to be effective and exchangeable. This feature is the foundation of *speaking about* matters, which we are constantly improving and making it more and more efficient. This feature evolved to become the "reason" for inventing writing; the preservation of knowledge for the future or as history of the past. Presently it is the core and impetus of the information revolution.

3. Integrating what we hear or see in the others' speech into our language, thus accumulating and improving the quality of mental achievement. In order to do that speech evolved into language, and language turned speech into a means to organize thoughts and harmonize their presence in two or more minds.

4. The importance of differentiating between the correct and the incorrect choice. Animals do not debate their choice before deciding. They do instinctively what they consider the right choice. Humans, from the onset of humanity strove to know what to choose (this piece of stone or that one to make a wedge). Only three thousand years ago Thales of Miletus posed the question; how could I know if what I hear is correct or incorrect? He gave birth to logic as the grounds for making a decision. Two hundred year later Aristotle wrote his thesis on logic, differentiating, classifying, and analyzing all the logical approaches used by the human mind. We make choices all the time and now we do not pray for the gods to make those choices for us as our ancestors did.

Those four characteristics created a very different mind from the minds of the rest of the animals. Instead of a well-defined mind with known instinctual potentials and limitations, humans have minds that are different in evolving and utilizing their potentials intentionally. This is the basis for the individuality of our minds: we can choose the way and the degree of unfolding our genetic endowment. In fact, there are no criteria of right or wrong for unfolding our potentials, hence, we find the human mind susceptible to unlimited possibilities to grow, and generate all the distinctions mentioned above.

The individual differences in the human mind result in creating the obvious differences within the human race. Each individual, although sharing fundamentals with others, is defined by the way his mind functions. Contrary to the fact that the defining quality of animals is the makeup of their minds, humans define their minds, that is, the person owns his mind instead. Therefore, if "mind" is a metaphor of consciousness in humans, we should be talking about the psychological nature of consciousness. Because a person is defined by the way he experiences his world (his experience of consciousness), he demonstrates more than the totality of the activity of consciousness; he demonstrates his subjective way of integrating those activities. The psychological nature of a person is what distinguishes him from others and not his mind.

The human mind has evolved from a very elementary genetic mutation to a fully-fledged phenomenon. We should expect that human consciousness must have also evolved and "logically" conclude that humans do not have a consciousness but they have consciousnesses. This idea denotes that it is an inherent aspect in the genetic mutation that led to the species of homo-sapiens. We inherited genes that allow differences. One of the constitutionally acquired differences is the special need of human infants for parental care. In animals, infants need parental care for protection, sustenance, and learning a few skills, but the rest of their needs are inherited and take little but fixed time to naturally come through. In most animals, this period of parental care is a fixed period for all offspring, standardized in the way it takes place, and shorter than in humans.

The history of the human race reveals that parental care of infants changed substantially over the millennia. It was shortest when humans were food gatherers, increased when hunting was added. Every time the method of food production became more complex, like in agriculture and industry, the period of child care and stay within the family unit extended. The human subject is born with physical and mental endowment, but they are not enough to make him adequate to deal with the ever changing demands of his society. Parental care in humans came to be more sophisticated over time in order to serve more than the purpose of protecting the child till he is capable of taking care of himself physically. The period of parental care in humans is a period of rearing a child and raising him to be a person in society of persons (in animals, parental care is decided by the time needed for the instinctual potentials to be fully active).

During the period of parental care the child's personal constitutional endowment is exposed to external forces, in the form of the parents' wishes for those inherent potentials of the child. Parents have a major role in molding their child's potential and forming it to fit their own ambitions and societal expectations. Therefore, the final brain product of the child is an expression of several known and quasi-known factors in his upbringing, environment, parental input, personal experiences, and a few more, in addition to his genetic setup. The proper term to the final product is the *psychological* nature of the individual. This feature gives subjectivity and qualia a very different meaning. They are not characteristics or intrinsic parts of human consciousness or the object of consciousness; they are the natural result of the psychological nature of that particular individual. Each art critique has his own view of what he is critiquing.

It is useless to aspire to know all that is there in the neural makeup of the human brain, or generate the unlimited diagrams of the interconnectedness of the neurons in that brain, because, after all is said and done, they represent the person's choice to make the functions of the nervous system generate his own personal consciousness. Besides, consciousness in humans is a small fraction of our mental life, because the impact of upbringing on the formation of the individual's psychological makeup happens only in his awareness, and not in consciousness. They happen before his consciousness could conceive of it (in layman terms they happen unconsciously). The evidence to that is the individual's capacity to imagine experiences that he did not get into, learn without practice, comprehend without analyzing matters, think, create without previous knowledge, and all that under the regulation of his psyche and without the involvement of consciousness.

In other words: *Consciousness does not have a neural match, the brain does not generate a consciousness equivalent, and the human subject is not a phenomenon of embodied brain. The human subject gives meaning to all those elements; his personal meaning. What those elements generate, whether they exist separately or do not happen if there is no interacting between them, is meaningless unless a human claims his ownership of them. The human subject gives an identity to the neural activity, its mental manifestations, and its particular constitutional prospective, that is, they are him.*[5]

THE PSYCHOLOGICAL AND THE NEUROLOGIST

Neurologists found consciousness an enigma (chapter two) because any way they approached it led them to the conscious-person whom they called the self. They did not have a neurological explanation to the formation of the self. Firstly, because the self is only definable by non-physical attributes of the person like character, morality, temperament, etc. Secondly, the individualistic nature of the psyche prevents them from making general functional or structural judgement of its neurological base. Thirdly, neurologists are not as prepared like psychologist to think of the person psychologically, that is, to see him outside the deductive way of thinking that is always geared toward causal explanations.

This last point is important because in the next three chapters I will deal with this issue extensively, based on an unfamiliar conception of the unconscious, which Freud formulated but discarded because of its unusual psychical nature. His exploration of the unconscious as repressed conscious material veiled another unconscious that is not repressed and is present in consciousness but *aconcsiously*, a concept which he puzzled about but finally managed to leave the clues to its solution. I will argue in chapter five that the real Freudian discovery was not the unconscious but what is better called the aconscious.

NOTES

1. A preliminary difference between awareness and consciousness is that the former generates a response without mental equivalents, and the latter, though instigated by awareness, goes further to become a mental event. Awareness of hunger moves the animal to hunt and eat, but in a human it generates a series of mental entities that the person considers before responding to his need, because humans are aware of awareness. The awareness of awareness creates consciousness.
2. Could consciousness of death be what generated replication as a solution? These ideas are of special interest to compare with Freud's theory of the polarity of life and death in his theory of *Trieb*.
3. There are reasons to ask those questions, in spite of having no answers to them. The most threatening attitude to thinking in human sciences (ideographic sciences) is foreclosure on ideas to avoid investigating other ideas. Talking about absolute matters like absolute consciousness or knowledge (contentless consciousness) sound unscientific and is unscientific till now. Questions about causes and effects are difficult to handle in matters of evolution, yet evolution would not be an issue without posing those questions. But, raising questions that are phenomenally correct even if we cannot answer them keeps the phenomenon alive for future investigations that might show that the questions we asked were incorrect.
4. Jaynes (1976) has an interesting hypothesis about the evolution of the human mind based on the genetic improvement in the neural link between the twos hemispheres of the brain (the bicameral brain). The evolutionary basis for his hypothesis explains few things if proven right. I admit that I tend to think he is right but my review of the neurological literature on that subject is limited and cannot support my views (his too) by real research.
5. There is a difference between the self as used by Damasio and to an extent by Edelman and Tononi and what I mean by the human subject. In neurological terms, self is an entity contained in a brain activity at a certain level of that activity. The human subject is what contains the brain that is neurologically a potential waiting for an instigator who owns it. This sounds like a metaphysical concept of the human subject, which it is. A brain that is more of potential than constitutional endowment is an organism that experiences and not just responds. It does not produce a self, but is produced in a self.

Chapter Four

Freud's *Project* and the Conception of Consciousness

While busy with Josef Breuer writing the *Studies on Hysteria*, Freud found the time to embark on a project to write a "psychology for the neurologists" (letter dated April 27, 1895). He was enthusiastic about the project as his correspondence with Fliess has shown. But, suddenly and just before completely finishing it, he shelved it until it was discovered over half a century later. Neither did he finish it nor did he get rid of it. Even the reason for taking on that project is baffling because there was no significant psychological movement at the time, or a need for a neurological explication to the psychology of that period (Brentano and Wundt). Nevertheless, the *Project* proves to be of significant importance in another way.

There is a solid agreement amongst analysts and the Freudian scholars that the *Project* embodies the blue print of the psychoanalytic discovery, albeit written in neurological terms. Freud's declared objective of the *Project* was to give psychology the scientific credibility of neurology as a branch of the medical sciences. In a remarkable way, the *Project* looks—in its final form—like a neurological document in search for a meaningful relation to the human subject in order to acquire credibility. Better, Freud described psychological phenomena in thorough neurological terms, which made neurology look credible as being capable to explain the evident.

Just before setting aside the *Project*, Freud summarized it in a letter (October 20, 1895) saying: "The three systems of neurones, the free and bound conditions of quantity, the primary and secondary processes, the main trend and the compromise trend of the nervous system, the two biological rules of attention and defence, the indications of quality, reality and thought, the state of the psycho-sexual groups, the sexual determinants of consciousness as a perceptual function—all fitted together and still fits together! Of course I cannot contain myself with delight." This is a very precise summary of over one hundred pages of neurological assumptions about the subject he dealt with in that project. It is a surprise and a revealing surprise that he called the *Project* his cross, and realized that he had to take another direction than neurology to achieve a *psychology of the subject.*

The *Project* was considered by many, as Strachey suggested in his introduction to its translation, to be a neurological document. Strachey specified several features that distinguished and separated it from the rest of Freud's works, which is defined to be the evolution and elaboration of the theory of catharsis. Yet he admitted that it (the *Project*) "contains within itself the nucleus of a great part of Freud's later psychological theories" (Strachey 1950, 292). I believe that this is true. However, I do not think Strachey realized its relevance to psychoanalysis by the way he had responded to it, probably because he had just finished with translating the whole Freudian text and was not able to relate the *Project* to his previously fixed ideas about psychoanalysis. He mentioned four main differences between the *Project* and the psychoanalytic theory. Those differences reflected Strachey's deep absorption in the work he had done on the main Freudian text, which made him biased against anything written in a different style or perspective, hence his disinterest in the content of the *Project*. His four objections have been proven later to be insubstantial by unbiased scholars.

The place of the *Project for a Scientific Psychology* (1950) in the *Freudian Cause*[1] is quite peculiar; it was meant to be a neurological thesis, presumably more science than psychology. He discarded the *Project* but did not get rid of it. He did not mention it again even when he wrote the history of the psychoanalytic movement (1914b). Those are indications that Freud did not acknowledge it as a link in the chain of his discoveries. Therefore, it would not be easy, but rather difficult, to show where the *Project* fits in the Freudian cause. Notwithstanding, after psychoanalysts were more familiar and experienced in the "logic" of psychoanalysis, they were able to read the *Project* without Strachey's lack of interest. There have been excellent and very convincing efforts done in that vein (Jones 1954; Pribram and Gill 1976), but their findings did not last. Despite a general agreement on its impact on the theory among the few analysts who read the *Project*,[2] there is very little interest in it, until now.

The *Project* was the first step Freud took outside his earlier neurological research, and it deceivingly looks unrelated to his budding clinical work with hypnosis, and without a definite or identified objective. Thus, reviving it now would interest only the scholarly psychoanalyst and undoubtedly the neuropsychologists. However, I give it a central position in discussing consciousness because the *Project* has the basis of the real theory of the *aconscious*. Aconsciousness is a human phenomenon that if properly presented and consequently understood could lead to a theory of consciousness in humans.

The *Project* looks—to the undiscerning eye—like a text that neither belongs to Freud's previous neurological work nor to his forthcoming psychological theory; the psychological theory that became the theory of psychoanalysis. It does not even relate *clearly* to anything that we know about the theory of catharsis, which Freud was formulating at the time he was writing the *Project*. However, examining the *Project* as *the odd work that should not have been*, reveals few significant things. It contains the seeds of a general theory of consciousness, which put an end to the theory of repression and the un-conscious. Lying dormant in the *Project* is a theory of consciousness that responds to the main problem that thinkers and neurologists are facing now when they talk about "the conscious." It also shows the difference between the functional and structural ways of thinking, which if not defined and noted it would create havoc in the research in consciousness. An additional value in the *Project* is the way it demonstrates Freud's way of thinking and his unusual sensitivity to the difference between thinking functionally and structurally. Bringing out those three features in the *Project*, and articulating them properly should reveal another but inactive theory of psychoanalysis (see Fayek 2013). In that inactive theory we could see that the underlying force behind discovering psychoanalysis was Freud endeavor to understand the peculiarities of consciousness in the psychoneurosis, and later in other human achievements.

THE SEEDS OF A GENERAL THEORY OF CONSCIOUSNESS

Freud's interest in consciousness was not an accidental step in his long and difficult trip to discovering psychoanalysis; it was the right first step that corrected a previous wrong one. In 1897, Freud abandoned hypnosis and developed an interest in advancing toward a theory of psychopathology and psychotherapy by just listening to his patients; use free association to discover what hypnotism used to uncover. Point in fact, and literally speaking, *Freud abandoned the unconscious as the area of research and made consciousness his venue to the exploration of the unconscious*. We know now that he abandoned that route because the unconscious separate from the conscious was *meaningless*. Two years prior to stopping the use of hypnosis, he embarked on the *Project*. The way it was written seems to have been an answer to an implicit question: *could he build a theory of the process that creates repression (a psychological theory of repression) using the terminology of a science that has a clear and acknowledged terminology, for example, neurology?* Could he find a neurological foundation to the anticipated psychological theory?

The *Project* was to build a psychological theory using the language of neurology. Like both Edelman and Tononi, and Damasio too, Freud the neurologist wanted to start from neurology, which he knew, to psychology which he vaguely knew. But this is as much as Freud has in common with the contemporary schools of functionalism in the field of consciousness. The difference is that Freud did not use the science of neurology to define a psychical entity like the self, as Damasio, for instance, tried. Freud wanted to use a science (neurology) to improve another science (psychology). This difference is better put like this: functional theories of consciousness were matching brain to mind or mind to self, while Freud was matching consciousness in neurology to consciousness in psychology.

One of Freud's objectives in the *Project* was to have a quantitative theory of mental functioning. His *Project* is anomalous in that sense: he left what he was seriously involve in and wrote a *Project* that was neither related to the subject he was engaged, nor pointed to what he later dedicated his life for. He defined his endeavor in the *Project* saying (letter dated May 25, 1895), "to examine what shape the theory of mental functioning takes if one introduced quantitative consideration, a sort of economics of nervous forces, and second, to peel off from psychopathology a gain for normal psychology. Actually, a satisfactory general conception of neuro-psychotic disturbances is impossible if one cannot link it with clear assumptions about normal mental processes." His endeavors, as he stated, did not stem from whatever he was working on nor were they clearly related to anything he worked on in the future. However, Freud averred in that letter a clear allusion to his interest in psychology and consciousness, because he realized that it is more sensible to explore the functions of the normal mind to be able to understand psychopathology properly. Hence, the attempt to create a neurology for psychology is seen as unconsciously anticipating the failures in the theory of catharsis, the limitations of the findings of the repressed, and the need to correct all that.

His statement about the need to study the "normal" suggests that the neurologist in him had become more interested in mental functioning and needed a firm psychological theory to guide him through. It also implies that his work with hypnosis was not explaining things properly and the theory of psychopathology, which he and Breuer came up with, needed another theory to explain it; a theory of normal mental functioning.

THE *PROJECT*[3] AND THE CONTEMPORARY FUNCTIONAL THEORIES OF CONSCIOUSNESS

The *Project* is unusual because it is, in many ways, very similar to the contemporary documents of neurologists investigating consciousness. This suggests that despite the major advancement in neurology in the last century neurologists' interest in consciousness is—matter of fact—a curiosity about the brain: how come that they know so much about it but cannot have an answer to the two major problems of qualia and subjectivity, as they are central issues in consciousness? As we will realize, Freud started from a slightly different point of view but not foreign to what we discussed in the first two chapters. Yet that slight difference was a matter of essence.

The *Project* started by ascertaining that as movement in the physical world is initiated by a quantity of energy psychical activity should also be presumed the product of neural energy initiated by stimulation. The neural energy is regulated by the neural structure of the nervous system. He said: "The nervous system as an inheritor of the general irritability of protoplasm . . . makes use of this *Q* [quantity of excitation in the neurons] which it has just acquired, by giving it off through a connecting path to the muscular mechanisms. . . . This discharge represents the *primary* [my emphasis] function of the nervous system. . . . Here is room for the development of *a secondary* [my emphasis] function" (1950, 296). Although at that time, the concept of a neural synapse was not yet coined by Sherrington (1897), Freud knew of the neural activities that were later assigned to the synapses. He qualified them as contact-barriers that are permeable or impermeable depending on the *quantity or the intensity* of the excitation that has to pass through them. If the intensity does not reach a certain degree to pass it could accumulate until it reaches that degree, or it gets dissipated if not supported by another quantity of energy.

The concept of repression is a product of that model where a blockage in the course of releasing the cathexis indicates its repression. He deduced from this that blocking the innervation causes pain while releasing the catharsis generates pleasure. Freud later assigned this conception to the *primary process* and averred that this came to him from his clinical experience; particularly the loose and unspecified manners patients use to release those catharses.

Following this starter he presumed the existence of three types of neurons.[4] *Phi* neurons specialized in receiving stimuli emanating from the external world, and not transmitting them as a flow but in quantities he called later *periodic* transmitting. The *psi* neurons are dedicated to receiving the endosomatic stimuli, which are the sensing of the variations in the somatic intensities—the *homeostatic balances*. They too have the quality of periodicity. The third are the *omega* neurons, or the *W* neurons, which are assigned for perception. We will later see those distinctions in Freud's theory of consciousness, because the omega neurons were connecting the sensory organs with cortical-sensory zones of the brain.

He followed those assumptions by several related ones; the most significant was the two types of the *psi* neurons. One is stimulated by endosomatic sources that generate excitements equivalent to states of "instinctual need," like hunger and thirst. This excitement—in humans—requires an extended dependence on the response of the external world. The *psi* neurons of that type create in the subject (infant) a *demand to connect* with the external world if a discharge is required, or as he said: "this path of discharge acquires a secondary function of the highest importance, that of *communication*" (1950, 318). At that point of elaborating his neurological model he faced the problem of consciousness in an unexpected way. Several important questions arose: how does the infant sense the depletion of a vital substance for the endosomatic stimuli excite their specific *psi* neurons? What makes the infant cry when the level of dehydration in his body increases? Does the infant become just aware or become conscious of that need?

Freud addressed this problem tentatively by saying that the *psi* neurons transmit the endosomatic excitation in periods to the *phi* system of neurons and they would be felt as if they are external stimulation—the type that creates consciousness through perception.[5] *This tentative answer is the seed of the extremely central but vague process of representation; the endosomatic presence in the mind as a mental occurrence*; "*Vorstellung*." Facing this issue and trying to find a neurological solution to it was very significant. It later became one of a few points of departure from the catharsis theory and an important process in another theory (Fayek 2012). It is a cardinal argument about consciousness at the present time.

At a certain point, Freud sensed that the *Project* led him to a theoretical problem. Both the external stimuli that excite the sensory organs thus initiating consciousness, and the endosomatic excitations, which are neurologically mute, and have no organs to sort them, activate the same nervous system. However, smell and taste are different because of the sensory organs that react to their different stimulation, while hunger and thirst are homeostatic imbalances and sensing them is not different enough neurologically to explain their distinction. The assumptions of general quantitative neural innervation of consciousness proved inadequate, because it does not explain the change from quantitative excitations of the sensory organs into qualitative perceptions like smell, lightness, etc., while the endosomatic stimulations which have no organs to define them could still be felt differently as hunger, thirst, etc.

Awareness of the external world is qualitative and specific by virtue of the specialized organs that respond to it. Consciousness, in that case, is a manifestation and a function of awareness, and could be qualified as perception. On the other hand, the impact of the endosomatic stimuli on the brain comprises intensities, pressures, and quantities of demands of homeostatic nature; they are not sensed differently, as nourishment or rest or sleep. Freud made a simple but key distinction between endosomatic stimuli and the exosomatic ones. He said that we can avoid or seek the external stimuli but when it comes to the endosomatic: "They [stimuli] only cease subject to particular conditions, which must be realized in the external world" (Freud 1950, 297). The conditions that influence those stimuli do not produce awareness, thus, they do not produce consciousness. Nevertheless, they produce "something" that can only be referents to what the stimulus demands from the external world. The stimulus remains unidentified and *aconscious* in spite of its persistence, until the caregiver responds to what it generates to get communicated and provides its needed substance. The referents they generate stand to represent them. We should underline here that the two types of neurons—the *phi* and the *psi*—could have been flawed assumptions from Freud, but they make sense in differentiating between *perception* of the external and the *representation* of the endosomatic stimuli.

His comment about this distinction is quite revealing. He said: "We might then conjecture that it might actually be our systems *phi* and *psi* each of which had assumed one of these primary obligations. The system *phi* would be the group of neurones which external stimuli reach, the system *psi* would contain the neurones which receive the endosomatic excitations. In that case we should not have *invented* the two [classes], *phi* and *psi*, we should have *found* them already in existence" (Freud 1950, 303). However, this was enough reason for Freud to abandon the *Project*,[6] just before being so close to completion. *He realized that he created a psychology for the neurologists when he intended to create a neurological or a scientific foundation for psychology.* It was Freud's first step toward the discovery of psychoanalysis, a new psychology for the human subject and a theory of his aconscious. Neurology was a backdrop for a number of intuitions (inductively reached) which needed to be anchored in some solid knowledge. Neurology in the *Project* was an early metaphor for a very auspicious discovery; therefore, when he neared its end he was ready for the real thing: psychoanalysis.

In a heuristic attempt to find a theoretical model for mental phenomena Freud came to *the distinction between endosomatic and exogenous stimuli, in terms of responding to each. He added to the issue of quantity to the element of quality in the form of pleasure and pain, thus put consciousness right in the theory.* To wit, Freud used neurological denotations to reveal psychical connotations and to have the right starting position to identify the conscious.

Freud had another quite revealing statement in the *Project*. After developing his neurological system, he said: "*every* psychological theory, apart from what it achieves from the point of view of natural science, must fulfil yet another major requirement. It should explain to us what we are aware of, in the most puzzling fashion, through our 'consciousness'; and since this consciousness knows nothing of what we have so far been assuming—quantities and neurones—it should explain this lack of knowledge to us as well" (Freud 1950, 307–308). The statement underlines two points. Firstly, psychology is not the science of just what we could become aware of. Endosomatic stimuli do not turn into awareness and become conscious material as the external stimuli do, yet they affect the same nervous system that initiates consciousness. There must be a point when they both meet, because they are both products of the same type of innervation. Although consciousness knows nothing about those "noetic" mental activities, they are still part of the province of psychology. As he said, they do not cease to stimulate until they are actualized externally. Therefore, a psychological theory has to account for what is *aconscious* as a psychoanalytic theory has to have a place for consciousness in it.

The second point is a very significant matter, not only to psychology but also to neurology: *is consciousness a function that brings the external world to the subject's mind, or is there a structural potential in the nervous system that turns excitations of the external world into consciousness*? Is the pressure of the stimuli the reason for human consciousness, or is the potential for consciousness a precondition for the stimulus to have an effect? Freud's statement raises those two germane questions. If consciousness is a precondition for stimulation, and endosomatic stimulation exists, then we have to *recognize the existence of a consciousness that is not conscious*. This paradoxical formula has taken another form later in the Freudian theory when he said that *everything that is repressed is unconscious but not all that is unconscious is repressed* (1923). It is easy to see in Freud's two statements, with thirty-eight years between them, how he has been struggling with the problem of a *unified theory* of the conscious and the unconscious all that time. Freud showed in this heuristic endeavor that he reached the edge of the difference between a theory that is dedicated to cause-effect formulations, or the reason for things to happen (functional), and a theory of the processes of things happening (structural), that is, how they happen when they do.

The *Project* had the seeds of *another* implicit theory within the theory of catharsis, which should have replaced it (Fayek 2013). This other theory of psychoanalysis was a project in the making from the time Freud started the *Project*, hence its beginnings in the *Project* were unnoticed when we found it in 1950. The *Project* was introduced to psychoanalysis (by the translating team) as an afterthought instead of being the very starting thought, and was positioned outside the *main canonized text*. Moreover, belittling its clinical value has distracted the psychoanalysts from its major breakthrough ideas, and has not attracted the attention of the non-clinical psychoanalysts either.

The *Project* is seldom considered part of the evolution of psychoanalysis. The reason, in my opinion, is double fold: first it was not related to the clinical field, which the therapeutic endeavor had a priority over anything else in psychoanalysis. Secondly, the Freudian doctrine is not a theory of the unconscious as is commonly thought; it is a *theory of the psychical in its dialectical meaning*, that is, the way the endosomatic stimulus emerges and evolves to become a psychological event and different from its basis in the body. The *Project* comprised consciousness in its fabric. This fact sheds light on the struggle Freud had with the concept of the unconscious every time he tried to think of it as a separate identity (Freud 1912, 1915c, 1923, 1940).

When we get to that struggle (chapter five), it will reveal the importance of knowing certain things about consciousness first, if he wanted to understand the unconsciouses. It will also show the significance of the *systemic unconscious* (*Ucs.*) when we put consciousness in a different context than the context of the theory of catharsis, or in contemporary psychologies. Freud's feeble and inadequate articulation of that aspect of the concept has caused his doctrine to be an easy target for rash criticisms. *Freud's real theory is a thoughtful and momentous attempt at discovering the particulars of human consciousness and its source, and the means by which it emerges in the form of psychical phenomena.*

We have to accept at this stage of examining the place consciousness in Freud's doctrine that things are not definite, clear, or mature enough to take a critical position from them. In the *Project* Freud was of two opposite minds regarding consciousness. One is that consciousness does not register everything that happens to the subject, like the endosomatic imbalances, somatic changes, and neural processes; thus, those facets should be considered unconscious. They happen and influence the brain but they are "unconscioused."[7] The second is consciousness as a separate entity that has nothing to do with endosomatic stimulation and should be understood—that is, if possible—as an independent psychical entity. This way consciousness became more confusing because if considered a function of perception, which is a lower level of neural activity, it would not account for the complexities of the mental processes that are the province of the cerebral cortex. Quality is another problem: it is not an attribute of perception or *phi* neurons (it does not come from outside) because consciousness is mainly a product of the cerebral cortex and not just the sensory motor areas. At the same time Freud says: "During perception the *phi* and the *psi* systems are in operation together; but there is one psychical process which is no doubt performed exclusively in *psi*—reproducing or remembering—and this, speaking generally, is without *quality*" (1950, 308). Even the attribute of quality could not be considered a privileged property of consciousness either.[8]

THE FUNCTIONAL AND THE STRUCTURAL IN THE *PROJECT*

As a psychologist, I have to underline a neglected point in the status of psychology, which relates, in a way, to the *Project* for a psychology for the neurologists. Psychology has always had some theories to explain psychical phenomena. It had associationism as a theory of perception, behaviourism to explain stabilities in the field of actions, pragmatism for motivation, the gestalt theory which is still the foundation of understanding mental processes, even used psychoanalysis to explain unfamiliar psychical manifestations. Nevertheless, *psychology, until now, has no general theory of the psycholog-*

ical: *What is what we call psychical or psychological*?[9] Freud's interest in consciousness and psychology as its basic science was never ended or shelved with the *Project*. He continued to puzzle over the place of consciousness in psychoanalysis. Whatever the analysts looks for has to be mainly in the conscious material the patient provides, and in the analyst's conscious understanding of it. If there is unconscious material to reach for it will always be through conscious processes. With properly positioning consciousness in the Freudian doctrine we could possibly get to that general theory of psychology.

The two systems of neurons, *phi* neurons and *psi* neurons, are different in the way they discharge their innervation. The *phi* neurons (responding to external stimulation) discharge their innervations without much resistance in the synapse, and once the discharge happens they return to their original state and are ready to receive new stimulations. The *psi* neurons (responding to the endosomatic stimulations) are not permeable; the discharge is not entirely a matter of the quantity of innervation. When the discharge of their innervation happens they maintain an impression (mnemic trace, Damasio's map) of that innervation.

Freud realized that neurons of both systems are morphologically the same. He then showed one of the characteristics of his thinking (discussed in the next section of this chapter). He concluded that the difference is not in the neurons but in the innervations of the *psi*, that is, he shifted from what seems to be the thesis to its antithesis; thus he found the answer. Freud recognized that "during perception the *phi* and *psi* systems are in operation together; but there is one psychical process which is no doubt performed exclusively in *psi*—reproducing or remembering—and that is, speaking generally is *without quality*" (ibid. 308). But because the *psi* system has no contact with the external world, but could receive innervation only from the biological changes in the body-cells and some peripheral stimulation from the system *phi* at the same time, he postulates the existence of the third system. The system Omega was dedicated to *perception* alone and became the neurons that create *conscious sensations*.[10]

Innervation creates a change that corresponds to the state of stimulation. He called that change *Affect* (affekt). The origin of that idea is that stimulations, whether external or internal, instigate only one of two reactions: pleasure or pain. Affect, thus, reflects the state of mind the stimulus has instigated in order for the discharge to happen. Affect regulates pleasure and pain by managing the accumulation and the discharge of their innervation. The accumulation of dissatisfaction causes pain and the release of that pain causes pleasure, as the repetition of satisfaction regenerates it. Freud dealt specifically with the issues of the discharge of innervation. He concluded that discharge of innervation originating from the external world, which is the source of extensive stimulation, requires more permeability between the neuron to allow more discharge and avoid over cathecting, and most of all to give the nervous system the ability to deal with the continuous flood of stimulation emanating from the external world. Discharge of endosomatic stimulation suggests that its neurons (if we could say so) are impermeable; they could preserve innervation and endure more accumulation before discharge. This feature is dictated by the fact that endosomatic stimulation is mainly chemo-hormonal and there are no receptive organs that could sort it out, and its satisfaction is always in the external world. Thus, it has to endure periods of delay in discharge due to the nature of satisfaction.

This conception of affect had significant implications on the *Project* (and later on the theory of psychoanalysis in general). He formulated a hypothesis about affect and memory in which the experience of pleasure and pain could be compulsively repeated. This notion implies that affect is *also* a state of wishing to repeat the sensations of pleasure and to avoid pain. But what concerns us here is the role of affect in the experience of consciousness. Freud stated that the cycle of the increase and decrease of the intensity of the endosomatic stimulus is the harbinger of consciousness. Consciousness in this condition is without content or a subject, but it is not simple awareness of comfort or discomforts either. The propensity to discharging the innervation is a state of wishing, that is, wishing as an affective state.

Before moving from this point to the next we have to recognize that Freud's conceptions and concepts of affect, innervation, external and internal stimuli, etc., are all structural. They do not denote specific entities but abstraction that does not hamper exploring their concrete nature further, if needed. The clear example to that is talking about the difference in the innervation between the *phi* and *psi* systems instead of differentiating between their neurons.

Although Freud at that stage of working on the *Project* was not, in anyway, aware of the full extent of his intuition, we can—at this stage of exploring and condensing the *Project*—underline in a limited way the relevance of that intuition to the theory of consciousness.

The system *psi* generates wishes that have no defined object to bind the affect to, while *phi* system deals with objects that exist separately from the subject and could be wished for. The affect of the wish for an external object could bind it to it. The *psi* wish creates fantasmic objects and create representations of them in tentative arbitrary trials, thus it resorts to approximations and partial appropriateness. Those attempts are the foundation of primary processes in the metaphors (condensation) and in the metonymies (displacement). Any *mental activity* created under the conditions of the primary processes has no chance to become conscious because fantasmic objects are contentless objects, they are representations. A toddler who is toilet trained has a fantasmic idea about what he is getting trained to regulate its release. He searches for an object to represent "that thing." A variety of things and ideas are there that he could latch that thing to, and the choice amongst them would be arbitrary depending to an extent on the suggestion the caregiver is giving: precious, gift, bad, relief, power, etc.

The external stimuli are identifiable and the discharge of affect would be direct and aimed at an existing target. Avoiding or seeking the object is possible and the system is more permeable and binds the affective energy to its specific target. Most of the reactions to the external world are cognitive and do not carry subjective psychical values. They do not acquire the subjective quality of cognition unless and until they find an endosomatic object suitable to bind with. The wish in the *psi* system is different and particularly important to explore. The wish for a nap is a vague thing to a toddler. The energy level law that creates that wish to nap and the endosomatic stimulation for relaxing are unbound, therefore the search for a suitable object to latch and bound the wish to nap to is different, because there is no limitations on preferring one object to the other.

The *psi* system deals with endosomatic stimuli, which are mainly chemohormonal changes. Those changes have no means to identify their objects endosomatically. It relies on the *phi* system (the caregiver) to provide that *object* in the external *world* (see Freud's previous statement about the two systems functioning together). The neural system of *psi* is impermeable and innervation does not discharge spontaneously. However, the *phi* system does not have or guarantee the proper object for the *psi* system; it might not provide the exact object for the affective wish. Therefore, the system might bind the cathexis of the affect to any object that it could fall upon (the thumb, the edge of a blanket, a pacifier, etc., as substitute for the real wish for the original object of the breast). Those substitute objects do not satisfy the *psi* wish in reality, and more often the connection would likely break and change. Hence, the search for the right object done by the system *psi* is tentative and Freud called the process *primary* (primary process as defined in the *Project* is: "Wishful cathexis to the point of hallucination [and] complete generation of unpleasure which involves a complete expenditure of defence are described by us as *psychical primary processes"* (ibid. 326–327).

The endosomatic stimuli are unavoidable; therefore, they constitute a special condition. They put pressure on the mind to attain its attention and reaction. What the brain can do with that pressure (in humans) is to represent the pressure in order to get the attention of the caregiver. Representing an endosomatic stimulus does not make it conscious. This observation and formulating it in this way attests to the existence of the logic of the concept of *Trieb* in the *Project*. Furthermore, the distinction Freud made put him face to face with another fundamental discovery that took twenty more years to be articulated properly. He said: "the omission of consciousness does not leave the psychical events unaltered but involves the omission of the contribution from [system *w*, the system of perception]" (1950, 311). There is enough in those distinctions to expect the emergence of a concept like *Trieb* but not the way Strachey translated it by *instinct.*[11] This intuition and the idea of the transformation of something originary into a by-product were the basis of several of Freud's theoretical discoveries like narcissism (1914a) and the concept of after effect (1918). He made a very clear-cut statement about that as he said: "no sexual experiences produce any effect so long as the subject is ignorant of all sexual feelings—in general that is, till the beginning of puberty" (1950, 333). They were also the foundation for the two dualities in Freud's *Trieb* theory or sex/ego instincts and life/death instincts.

We have to stop at what seems to be a minor concept in the *Project*, because missing its significance would not allow understanding later of the concept of aconsciousness. Wishes are subject to frustrations and failure to satisfy. The reaction to not gratifying them is repressing the wish. Repressing a wish for something in the external world is mainly achieved by repressing its material objects. The external stimulus, such as the smell of the mother's milk, evokes the wish for a "particular" breast and not any other object. The affect of that wish is bound to its object, and Freud identified those relationships as object-related. Thus, the infant would repress his wish for the breast and replace it with another object. This is the repression Freud talked about in his early theory of psychopathology, where the hysterical patient would repress the content of the objectionable psychical wish and the wish remains void of an object. Consciousness in that case would have a *gap* in its normal functioning.

Repressing a wish related to an endosomatic stimulus is a substantially different process. There is no object for the endosomatic stimulus that could be avoided by that kind of repression. The endosomatic wish cannot be repressed, thus its representations become the target of the repression. In the language of the *Trieb*, its aim and its object become the target of repression, but, because the aim of the wish is vital, persistent, and never ceases, repression is directed mostly to its object, which is the source of generating the representations. Consciousness in that case seems to have unusual detours that reveal the effort of avoiding the "repressed." It took Freud twenty years to come up with the distinction between those two types of repression, when he gave them different denotations: primary repression for repressing the endosomatic wish and its representations, and repression proper for the repression of the content of the wish for something in the external world (Freud 1915b).

The distinction between the two types of representations and the corresponding types of repression is a basic distinction between functionalism and structuralism. After discarding the *Project*, Freud directed his attention to functional entities that could explain or be explained like defence mechanisms, repression of libidinal urges, resistance, the unconscious as a function of repression and as a reservoir of objectionable impulses, etc. It took him two decades to reach a "turning point"[12] in his theoretical formulations. He revised his three main concepts of repression (as mentioned above), the unconscious, and *Trieb*. He also introduced the concept of narcissism, which changed the libido theory radically. He embarked on reformulating his functional theory into a structural theory, that is, instead of a theory of functional entities to a theory of the structural nature of those entities (*Trieb* is an inclination not a content, psychical processes, *systemic* unconscious, and a clear distinction between consciousness/precociousness and the aconsciousness). The structural nature of the theory was a most fundamental proposition that saved psychoanalysis from stagnating at functional links between causes and effects. All those divisions bring us back to the two types of consciousness mentioned above, the structural nature of Freud's arguments in the *Project*.

FREUD'S WAY OF THINKING

Psychology—by definition—is the science of consciousness; whether expressed in cognitive functions, or manifested in behaviour. It is the science of consciousness, but only in its active, evident, realized, and displayed form. Freud gave a comprehensive neurological framework for how consciousness—in terms of its psychological nature—generates in the brain, but he also acknowledged that some psychical material exist *in a state of unconsciousness*, which contributes to the processes that leads to consciousness. The most intriguing in his acknowledgment is expecting a psychological theory of unconsciousness to explain the processes that lead to consciousness, and if that is not possible, to explain the difficulty in doing so. This puzzlement is key to understanding Freud's dismissal of the *Project*, and his interest in a theory of psychology of the subject, instead of a psychology for the neurologists or a psychology of the brain.

He tried to give a comprehensive psychological theory based on neurology. He faced the three problems that the contemporary neurologists are still facing: qualia, subjectivity, and the unconscious. He suggested a neurological explanation for qualia but it was merely tentative, and was not verified later in modern neurology. Subjectivity was not central in his neurological inquiries at the time. Instead of going into the loop of which science explains the other, he realized, right away, that the problem is in what Einstein identified almost forty years later: "*No problem can be solved from the same level of consciousness that created it.*" Thus, the solution of the problem is to study consciousness afresh: it is not an entity that could be referred to another as its sign, but an attribute of the subject who is the topic of the investigation. *Better, the problem is the human subject and not his consciousness*. His psychical life—a very particular form of mentation—comprises an aspect that is neither conscious, nor available to consciousness in order to allow us to examine it, yet without it we are unable to fathom that subject properly.

At the time Freud gave up on the *Project*, he was beginning to explore the hysterical patients' denial of being conscious of what is causing their pathology, despite the clarity of what they deny. He used the term unconscious, a term that was hinted to by one or two philosophers before. He even showed a very early insight about what was awaiting him to discover: aconsciousness. He starts off that exceptionally challenging voyage in the *Project* by making distinctions in the concept of the unconsciousness, which were not properly noticed or spotted by others.[13] The *Project* has signs of an early attempt at a theory comprising the conscious and the unconscious, but it was still too early to move from the existence of anything beyond consciousness to a vague acknowledgment of that entity, and from it to the injudicious concept of the repressed, to the different states of unconsciousness, and finally to a true theory of aconsciousness.

Psychology, in the nineteenth and twentieth centuries studied consciousness separately from the unconscious. It failed to have a theory or even an incomplete one of that psychical entity. Early common psychoanalytic preoccupations, on the other hand, focused on the unconscious ignoring consciousness. That also resulted in the inadequate psychoanalytic concept of the unconscious as repressed consciousness. A theory of the psychological would not have been possible without the unison activity of consciousness and unconsciousness, because as we will be shown later, neither could exist if the other did not actively exist.

Freud's first ambition was to build a psychology or to discover the psychology of consciousness. He said, "psychology which has always been my distant, beckoning goal, and which now, since I have come upon the problem of neuroses, has drawn so much nearer" (May 25, 1895). Yet, he was almost destined to discover the mental in its dormant, disguised, and latent states, or in the state of unconsciousness. That is what he was known for. However, how could we reconcile Freud's basic interest in psychology and dedicating his search to the nature of the unconscious? The reason to query this matter is Freud's distinct approach to problematic issues. He resorted, and in a natural way, to the antithesis in any thesis of anything whose synthesis he wanted to research. The antithesis—dialectally speaking—shed more light on the thesis and the outcome of their interaction to create their synthesis. He was unable in the *Project* to formulate a theory of consciousness (both neurologically and psychologically), so he resorted to exploring the phenomena of unconsciousness. This feature in Freud's thinking prevails in every step he took in building his theory of psychoanalysis. He thought that if *the conscious is a problem, then studying the unconscious might solve that problem*. This is a main dialectical fiber in Freud's text, which Ricoeur (1977) and Politzer (1928, 1994) underscored and emphasized.

Freud as a thinker also looked for solutions to wrong ideas more than he searched for the right ones. He learned a few functional things about the psychopathology of hysteria from using hypnosis and bypassing repression. However, he realized very early that this venue, though it still had a few new things to offer, was leading to an impasse about understanding the structure of psychopathology. He discovered that hysterical symptoms resulting from repressing or expelling from consciousness unacceptable wishes, fantasies, thought, etc., are still not understandable even after removing repression. He also concluded that bringing the repressed back to consciousness *is supposed* to result in the disappearance of symptoms. It did, but the patient still remained "sick." The link between psychopathology and treatment of hysteria proved to be uncertain; he anticipated that the real impasse was in the futility of studying the repressed while the patient is not fully conscious.

For a time he believed that psychopathology is distortion of consciousness caused by repression, but he wanted to know why repression changes consciousness differently in different psychoneuroses. The impasse was that a theory of repression does not explain the changes in consciousness that result from the specific psycho-pathology. He abandoned hypnosis and used the patient's speech while fully conscious (free association) instead. He realized that the *pathological process changes the person and the person changes his consciousness*. Freud aspired for something more than becoming a hypnotist; he wanted to know and explain how psychopathology changes the individual, and therefore he could theorize about the changing of consciousness.

Freud was a proficient dialectical thinker, and his way of dealing with the problem of consciousness is exemplary of this model of thinking. Most valuable of Freud's thinking was intuitive thinking, that is, inductive, reproductive, and not deductive. When he was still using hypnosis he thought about the relation between the normal and the abnormal. He kept moving from the abnormal to the normal and unexpectedly realized that the matrix of the event (psychopathology) is correct, but it lacks what could explain it: if a synthesis (psychopathology) is discordant with the theory of treatment (thesis) then the problem is in the antithesis which is what normalcy is. Better, if the theory of the abnormal is correct (thesis), and treatment (synthesis) is meant to make the abnormal normal and it fails, then the problem is in the antithesis (in what is considered normal). As a thinker, he turned the problem downside up. *What is normal?* He spent five years (1900–1905) studying the unconscious in normal phenomena: dreams, daily phenomena of minor conscious aberrations, sexuality in children, and jokes.

Shifting from the thesis to the antithesis gave Freud the freedom to think *inductively* regardless of the "bad" reputation that it is unscientific thinking.

Inductive thinking facilitated and inspired intuitions to come easily and reconstruct the field of investigation. For instance, the abundant stories by patients about sexual abuse by adults, without convincing material evidence to their validity or invalidity or the degree of their prevalence, encouraged Freud to consider the existence of sexual desires and fantasies in children that, as a source, generate those sexual stories. This way, he recognized and discovered and presented a catalogue of childhood sexuality (1905b). This same catalogue became a diagnostic system of adults' psychopathology. That discovery unravelled more than expected of the psychoneuroses. A great deal of the meaning of symptoms was embedded in childhood sexuality. Another benefit of the shift from the thesis to the antithesis was moving his attention from *what* and the *why* things happen to *how* they happen. After thinking of why or what happened in a sexual seduction he was freed to think of how childhood sexuality could generate those stories.

He stopped being distracted by the issues of content that initiate repression, and moved to knowing how repression happens; how does consciousness get split and part of it disappears in forgetfulness; as it seems. After reaching that point in his clinical practice he went back to a remarkably ingenious intuition he previously had in the *Project* (1950, 311) about the twofold consciousnesses (I will come to that in the next chapter). Freud was ready by then for a theoretical leap. After the five years between 1900–1905 (mentioned above) he turned back to his medical inclinations. During that time, he showed another sign of his way of thinking. Using inductive thinking more expertly he abandoned functional formulations that are supported by deductive thinking only. He became more interested in the structural nature of the phenomena he was working on. Explaining the dream as wish fulfillment is a functional explanation, but to describe a dream as the outcome of the dynamic interaction of the day residues, an infantile wish, and the workings of the primary process (condensation and displacement) is giving it structural meaning. A structural meaning deals with the core of the phenomena. Freud encountered some delay in finishing his "dream book" and wrote to Fliess saying: "I now also understand why in spite of all my efforts I have not yet finished the dream [book]. If I wait a little longer, I shall be able to present the psychic process in dreams in such a way that it also includes the process in the formation of hysterical symptoms" (January 3–4, 1899). It is obvious that Freud had his eyes on more than simple functional explanations of isolated psychical phenomena.

He spent a decade gathering and organizing psychical material from patients and building a psychopathological theory based on the content of that material. Then, almost suddenly in 1915, he changed direction and got interested in *the psychological processes* that produce such material; he wrote his three major metapsychological[14] papers in 1915, followed by three more in three years. The shift to the psychology of the main psychical processes in psychoanalysis produced a totally new theory of psychoanalysis.[15]

Mehlman (1970, 1976) concluded (from his reading of J, Laplanche), that Freud left us two structurally polemic fields, which keep struggling in dominating the field of psychoanalysis. One could easily be identified as a theory of causes and effects (functions), whereas the other theory is of structures and processes.[16] Freud evoked the concept *Trieb* to explain the ways urges effect the mental to create the psychical. Regrettably, Freud gradually ignored that *Trieb* is not a particular urge but the tendency of urges to create mental representations. For that reason, the Freudian theory as it evolved and expanded did not relinquish the functional approach completely, and the remnants of catharsis theory kept a functional taste lingering in the Freudian doctrine.

A structural theory deals with the grammar of processes; the implicit laws that organize them. The structure of a psychical phenomenon discloses the manner that a phenomenon was created. Therefore, a structural theory is the configuration of the laws of the phenomena. An example could clarify this point. A person who was entrusted with some money developed a compulsion to count the money repeatedly with continuous doubt in his counting. It could be said that he had a repressed *wish* to steal the money and did not trust himself. This kind of link between compulsivity and the repressed wish is functional, that is, the "cause" explains the effect. In a structural approach, the act of counting and doubting the count is one act (a structure) that states that stealing could have happened but it did not. The symptom—in that case—is seen as a *meaningful* act. The wish is irrelevant to the compulsive act of doing and undoing; it only gives the compulsive act a subject matter. The compulsion is structurally independent of the content of the act and could explain other acts of compulsion that look like they have a different content.

Freud was not able in the *Project* to use inductive thinking in dealing with consciousness for two reasons: the first, consciousness did not seem to be a thesis with a problem that could persuade Freud to look for its solution. It was considered to be self-evident, except for the philosophers of the nineteen century who were intrigued by the transcendence of awareness; the certainty of the awareness of awareness. Therefore, Freud was content with seeing consciousness as a separate entity that should be treated in isolation of the rest of the neurological issues he meant to deal with. He was a neurologist and not a psychoanalyst or a psychologist yet. The second reason, consciousness has an obvious functional quality manifested in its cognitive byproducts, which was impossible to ignore. It is a function of the effect of stimuli on the organism. Its structural nature did not come out until it was put in the context of the theory of the unconscious.

NOTES

1. Freud's legacy is based on both his text and the manner the text was written. It is not unusual that a text of that volume and nature would go beyond its author's intended intentions, because he could have tapped unintentionally into matters that were beyond his conception at the time. In that kind of text words carry more meanings than the author has meant. For that reason we should allow the Freudian text to tell us more than Freud had intended, albeit within the facts of what he said. As such, we could, and maybe should, consider psychoanalysis a "cause" more than a theory, and the Freudian Doctrine as a gateway to something that came to Freud but was left to us to cross and go beyond.

2. I do not know any training institute that includes the *Project* in its syllabus.

3. Freud's *Project* is not amenable to abridgment because it is an abridgment in its own right. The brief account I will try to provide is basic conceptions that showed Freud's preoccupation with the concept of consciousness, major intuitions that were developed later in his construction of the theory of psychoanalysis, notions of processes that should be underlined in advance to show their significance which came to him later, and a main issue: his structural thinking. This last issue if missed would make the *Project* merely an odd document within the Freudian general text, which it is not by any means.

4. This classification of neural cells is quite unacceptable now, after over one hundred years of discoveries in the field of the nervous system and the contemporary classifications of neurons. Nevertheless, Freud's primitive classification remains valid if we put it in context of a purely psychological theory: instead of types of neuron, we consider types of psychical functions. Responding to the external world (*phi*), reacting to endosomatic changes (*psi)*, and the function of perception, it could replace the flawed neurological classification. It also shows the *Project* as a psychological model more than being a neurological framework.

5. The infant does not perceive his hunger, neither the adult. Nevertheless, the idea of transforming the endosomatic excitation from internal to external plays a significant role in the process of representing the endosomatic stimulus in the mind; which is the crux of consciousness in the theory of the anconscious.

6. A few days after his very upbeat letter to Fliess (November 8, 1895), he reported that he had put the whole *Project* away to be looked at later, but it stayed where he had put it for over fifty years until it was discovered.

7. See 1950, footnote p. 308, where Strachey underlines Freud's usage of a verb in a different translation to English to mean "not allowed to become conscious," but also means not different from being repressed.

8. Notwithstanding all those difficulties, Freud made an extraordinarily suggestion regarding quality and consciousness that was neither picked up by psychologists, nor by neurologists, not even by psychoanalyst. He said about neural transmission: "I shall assume that all resistance of contact-barriers applies only to the transference of Q [quantity] but that the *period* [transference of neural charges happens in pulsations and not a flow] of the neural motion is transmitted without inhibition in all directions, as though it were a process of induction" (1950, 310). He referred quality to that new postulate. This point will reveal its significance when we come to discussing the issue of "representation." Following this reconfiguration Freud foresaw the cardinal problem of consciousness and where it should be positioned in psychoanalysis. He said: "According to an advanced mechanistic theory, consciousness is a mere appendage to physiologico-psychical process. . . . According to another theory, consciousness is the subjective side of all psychical events. . . . [in] the theory developed here . . . consciousness is the subjective side of one part of the physical processes; and the omission of consciousness does not leave psychical events unaltered" (ibid. 311).

9. Each religion as an entity generates an abundance of theories, but they are different from the *Generic Theory of Religion* that deals with the essence of religiosity.

10. This summary, like any other summary, would make it look like Freud was groping with his neurological model. In the text he is clear and steady moving from hypothecs to another and from one assumption to a conclusion. However, what makes his ideas seem a little disjointed in a summary is that Freud was presenting a neurological theory and was searching

for its psychological basis; contrary to what he intended when he started. We notice the same thing in Damasio's attempt at building a neurological model on psychological framework.

11. Freud said (1926, 200) that the concept of *Trieb* has no equivalent in other languages. Therefore, it is better to use it as is to avoid thinking of it as drive or somatic need.

12. Scholars of the Freudian doctrine agree that there was a turning point in his theoretical conception of psychoanalysis. They disagree on when and what was the most revealing changes of the turning points. I believe that it started in 1915 and continued till 1920 with his work "Beyond the Pleasure Principle" (1920).

13. Strachey says that Freud used the word *unbewussst* in that regard, which should be translated as "made unconscious" or unconscioused (1950, 308 fn.1). I am suggesting using aconscious instead because it means without the "means" to be conscious.

14. Strachey put together as papers on metapsychology Freud's three papers on "Instincts," "repression," and the "Unconscious." Those papers have *nothing* to do with metapsychology (topography, economy, and dynamics). They are three papers on the psychology of the three topics.

15. I explained that difference in another publication (Fayek 2013). I tried to show the limited potentials of the catharsis theory, and to account for the rich conceptions of the theory of psychoanalysis. I also showed the systematic and obvious (but unnoticed) links of those conceptions if considered outside the framework of the catharsis theory.

16. The model of the "structural" metapsychology of ego-psychology is not structural in the epistemological sense of the term. It should not be confused with structural theories that are founded on concepts of processes and not of entities and content. The id, in ego psychology, is the system that functions as the "reservoir of instincts" or *Trieben*. In a structural theory the *Trieben* are the originator of mental representations of the endosomatic stimuli and not a reservoir of anything.

Chapter Five

A Brief Account of the Theory of the Aconscious

"If Freud's discovery had to be summed up in a single word, that word would without any doubt have to be 'unconscious'" (Laplanche and Pontalis 1973, 474). This seems at first a valid statement, because the rest of Freud's ideas were only meaningful and internally interrelated due to the centrality of the unconscious in them all. What could raise some questions about the validity of this statement is the existence of three meanings of the unconscious (Freud 1915b) and the undecidedness amongst analysts on which of them they adopt. Opatow (1997) said: "We have no unified notion of the unconscious, even within psychoanalysis itself. This is evident when one considers that the concept of the unconscious is virtually coextensive with psychoanalysis as a whole, and that this whole divides into several separate schools. Does the unconscious comprise sexual drive derivatives, internal object relations, or narcissistic needs" (865).

The various meanings of the unconscious are a result of more than one line of advancement and progression in the theory, which had encouraged taking the latest definition as the one Freud certified at the end. The three definitions Freud provided were separate insights and distinctively independent conceptions of three different states of unconsciousness. Each insight produced and forced reformulation of the theory to tally it, and there is no obvious thread to link the three different formulations of the unconscious to different phases of theoretical maturation. Therefore, tracing the meaning of the unconscious in the theory will appear disorganized, because following a detailed scholarly exposition of Freud's thinking is required to do that, which would distract from the main point.

Unfortunately, Freud did not always acknowledge, properly, his intuitions and the major changes they made to the theory. He remained firmly captive of the model of the unconscious as the repressed, despite the failure of repression in explaining the richness of his clinical discoveries and the flood of new ideas his disciples brought to light. The repressed was the descriptive meaning of what is unconscious and remained the center piece of his theorizing in spite of its insufficiency.

THE THREE DIFFERENT ASPECTS OF THE UNCONSCIOUS

Freud's interest in the treatment of hysteria in the late nineteenth century was purely medical. His cooperation with Breuer (1882–1895) and the visit to Paris in 1896 were to learn more about hypnosis. Hypnosis as a method of treatment (without a theory of psychopathology) made him pay attention to *repressed conscious material* that played an important role in causing the hysterical conditions. However, his clinical experience made him realize that "the repressed" did not just cause the disease; it became the core of the formation of the symptoms. The symptom pointed to a diagnosis of the cause. Freud also realized that—after all—the unconscious was still inclined to transpire through the ordinary speech of the patient. The repressed manages to state its presence in consciousness despite repression. The ineffectiveness of hypnosis as a method of treatment, and the insights in the link between diagnosis and causation in psychical phenomena, made Freud abandon hypnosis by 1897 to rely completely on the patients' association. Free association and hypnosis before that gave the unconscious a *descriptive* meaning, that is, it was what is removed from consciousness but leaves its mark in the symptom.

Freud recognized the repressed in the symptom with little difficulty, although it still remained unconscious to the patient. He posed a new question: if repression repels something conscious out of it, what makes it still palpable in consciousness though it remains unconscious? The answer to this question came to Freud in an indirect way.

He spent four years—after abandoning hypnosis—examining and exploring what would be considered, at least in his time, banal phenomena (dreams, parapraxes, jokes, and other psychical phenomena). Those phenomena *have manifested forms and latent meaning*. Previously (in the *Project*) he made a distinction between the primary and secondary process in their role in creating psychical material. He eventually formed a solid conception of the working of the primary process in creating psychical phenomena like dreams and jokes. The working of primary process required distinguishing between the origin of the psychical phenomena and its manifestation; the basis of separating the manifest content from the latent meaning in dreams, and the joke, and the irony behind its innocent manifest expression. At that phase of his research, which was in its most elementary stage, he thought that repression uses the primary process to obscure latent meaning in the manifest content. The characteristics of the primary process—as he was able to identify—were very useful in reading in the symptom more of the disguised content. A new meaning of the unconscious was to emerge, however slowly.

After using this angle in studying dreams, parapraxes and jokes, and thinking about symptoms in the same vein, he realized that something was missing about sexuality, which should make the sexual "trauma" behind the symptom make sense. He could not apply the working of the primary process to include sexuality in symptom formation, because although its contribution to psychopathology was undeniable it did not seem to contain the meaning of the symptom. However, he noticed that sexual immaturity is a problem in the neurosis, revealed in the loose and sometimes ridiculous links between the sexual objects and sexual aims in those patients (1905b). He expected then that the primary process—condensation and displacement—must be operating somehow in that manifestation of sexual immaturity. Infantile sexuality gave him the solution to the place of sexuality in the neuroses. This was *the spark* he waited for to set the book on sexuality ablaze, as mentioned to Fliess in one of his letter (January 3–4, 1899). Most importantly, infantile sexuality enabled him to explain the frequent unverifiable reporting of sexual abuse in the childhood of those patients, and added to the picture the new concept of fantasy. The burgeoning discoveries of the role of infantile sexuality in psychopathology overshadowed most other theoretical interests for a period of time. Nevertheless, the unconscious still remained the container of the rejected and repressed,[1] or as Laplanche said: ". . . repression is sexuality, or the object of repression is sexuality" (1976, 27). It was infantile sexuality and not sexuality as such that was behind the hysterical symptoms and other aspects of the psychoneuroses.

Infantile sexuality forced the introduction of the concept of *Trieb* to the theory of psychoanalysis, because sexuality proved to be more than just the sexual urge. Two main changes to the theory ensued by the introduction of the concept of *Trieb.* The *first* was associated with the nature of the concept itself. This concept forced a distinction between responding to the endosomatic stimuli—the homeostatic needs—and reacting to the external world or the physical stimuli (note that Freud has come to the same idea in the *Project*, but because it was dropped it looked like a new insight). The endosomatic stimulus exerts pressure on the mind to react by representing it mentally (*Vorstellung*). Based on that simple and obvious observation, Freud found it imperative to revisit the concept of repression a few years later (1915b). He suggested and formulated the model of two types of repression, one that deals with the representations of the endosomatic stimuli, and one that deals with the external stimuli. He said: "We have reason to assume that there is a primal repression, a first phase of repression which consists of the psychical (ideational) representation of the instinct being denied entrance to consciousness, with it a fixation is established, the representative in question persists unaltered . . . due to the properties of the unconscious [replacement of external reality by psychical reality]" (1915b, 148). He called one "primal repression" and the other "repression proper."[2]

The *second* change was necessary because if we have two types of repression then infantile sexuality must be targeted by one of them; but which one? If so, what does the other repression repress? To shorten a long and complex process of theoretical changes that Freud went through in that regard I would say: *Trieb* forced a distinction between two repressions: primal repression and repression proper, and between *two corresponding unconsciousnesses one belonging to the endosomatic and the other relates to the exosomatic.*

Freud treated *Trieb* as a dual structure and not a unitary structure that could be defined as instinct or drive. His first *Triebhaft* duality was of self-preservation *Trieb* and a sexual *Trieb.* Infantile sexuality was characterized by the arbitrariness of the links between its aims and its objects. Therefore, as an endosomatic stimulus, its pressure on the mind is a complex matter and constitutes the rich background of the psychical life—normal and abnormal. The endosomatic stimulations (the *Triebhaft*) requires primal repression, because it is elementary and an originary stimulation. It is also unavoidable and the person has to respond to it. It should not enter consciousness as is, and has to undergo the process of representation to be material for mental activity.[3] The external physical stimulation does not need repression because it could be avoided physically if one so wished.

We come to examining the *two types* of repression. The distinction made by Freud led him to another very significant insight about the relationship between defence and the unconscious; an insight that remained, and still remains, hardly mentioned. He stated (1915b) that: "repression is not a defensive mechanism [eliminating from consciousness what threatens the ego] . . . until a sharp cleavage occurred between conscious and unconscious mental activities" (146). The separateness between what is conscious and what is unconscious is a prerequisite for the ordinary process of repelling from consciousness (repressing) to happen. The unconscious thus is predicated on a separation between those two mental activities, or what those two activities imply. Once again, to make a long story of theoretical struggle short, I would say that *a cleavage between the endosomatic need and its mental representation has to happen first in order for the work of primal repression to take effect.* Only after the mental representations are separated from the endosomatic stimuli by primary repression could repression proper act upon those representations. Thence, repression could be called a defence against the mental representation; what is repressed is not the endosomatic need but its representation and the representations of the original representation.

Repression until that time was the prototype of the unconscious, and the exemplary defence. But when that notion of defence was applied to defending the ego, other defences proved to be equally effective. Therefore, defence (*not repression as a defence*) became the prototype of the unconscious (Freud 1923), and repression was only one of the defences and defined as the process of repelling something from consciousness. Better, what was expelled from consciousness and became "un"-unconscioused was the repressed, but other effective defence mechanisms did not repress any of consciousness and still did not create unconsciouses. *It became clear that repression or any other defence mechanisms do not create the unconscious; it is the unconscious emergence of mental representations that generates all defence mechanisms.* Better though, defence mechanisms are functions of the work of the unconscious primary process.

It is important to introduce the concept of the preconscious at this point. Primal repression prevents the entrance of endosomatic to consciousness, awaiting turning it into a representation or mental material (hunger and satiation are represented by emptiness and fullness). At the same time there is material arising from responding to the external world and they are conscious. This material is what repression acts upon.[4] It expels it from consciousness. Therefore, we have to recognize the existence of another state of affairs that is neither totally unconscious (the representations) nor totally conscious (the repressed), which Freud called the system preconscious: *Pcs.* The preconscious is a link between consciousness and unconsciousness, in the sense that they both require the existence of the other to keep their usefulness to the subject.

First representation is thing-presentation, which could go into a process of creating representations of representations. Nonetheless, they are only material for fantasies, nothing more, like fantasies of emptiness and fullness. *For thing-presentation to find its way to consciousness it has to connect first with the caregiver's own fantasy about the same representation.* Only then it will find its word-personation; become material for communication. It will find the opportunity to link with the preconscious material; material that was originally conscious and stemming from the symbolic order of things. The repressed gets the inertia from the representation to return to consciousness. Better, the representation offers its affective energy to the affectless repressed event. Still, the link between the unconscious and consciousness through precociousness is dominated by the rules of the primary process. This fact defies the simplistic notion of the unconscious invading consciousness. It has to go through the preconscious and links with its material before being admitted to consciousness. Point fact, this is very fundamental in understanding consciousness.

Transposing unconscious material to the *Pcs./Cs.* does not make it disappear from the *Ucs.* system. It will still have its unconscious inscriptions or registrations. This important point explains two things: on the one hand the enduring nature of the unconscious and its continuous reappearance in the conscious material, using different preconscious contents. The other is that it shows the nature of the systems, *Ucs., Pcs./Cs.*, and their different effects on the same unconscious materials. *The system, not the psychical material, makes the difference; not the quality of what is repressed but which system will repress.*

The conception of unconsciousness as a *function* of defence mechanisms had a subtle weakness. In any functional relationship there is an implicit "cause-effect" link. Any causal relationship is subject to an imperceptible but serious logical defect. There is always the possibility that something else could be the cause of both components:[5] something creates the defence mechanism which is presumed to be the cause of the unconscious, or *something* instigates the unconscious which in turn produces the defence mechanism. As early as 1896, Freud defined repression as: "A failure in translation [from one psychic system to another]—that is what is known clinically as repression" (1896a). A few months later he said: "It is not sufficient to take into account the repression between preconscious and the conscious; we must also consider normal repression within the system unconscious itself. Very important, still very obscure" (Draft M, May 25, 1897). Freud was predicting the theoretical discovery he made two decades later: the two types of repression. Primal repression is censorship within the system unconscious of itself and keeps what is originally unconscious from entering the sphere of consciousness. The mental representation—as we mentioned above—would link with preconscious material and become subject to repression proper, that is, lowering the barriers within this material would produce conscious material that is confusing and does not accommodate the rules of the secondary process (1915a, 1917). When the unconscious was still the container of repudiated material the difference between the two censorships was explained in economic metapsychology; crossing the barrier depended on the strength of the repressed. But the work on dreams made Freud realize that this idea is flawed. Crossing the barrier in each of the two cases creates different psychical events. In dreams like "Autodidasker's" (1900, 298–302), the day's residues (*Pcs.*) had to be worked extensively by the primary process to disguise the unfulfilled wish (*Ucs.*). This is found in some psychoneuroses like fetishism, where the removal of the censorship between the *Ucs.* and the *Pcs.* does not reveal or change things much. In dreams like "The Burning Child's" (ibid. 542), the wish for seeing the son once more was fulfilled in a direct way, indicating a simple lowering of the censorship between the conscious wish and the preconscious. We usually encounter such direct expressions of the unconscious in hysterical neuroses.

The functional relationship between defence and the unconscious presumes tension between two forces: the power of the repressed and the strength of repression. However, Freud intuited the fallacy of that conception too as he said (1912): "We are accustomed to thinking that every latent idea was so because it was weak and that it grew conscious as soon as it becomes strong. We have now gained the conviction that there are some latent ideas which do not penetrate into consciousness, however, strong they may have become. Therefore, we may call the latent ideas of the first type *foreconscious* [preconscious], while we reserve the term *unconscious* (proper) for the latter type which we come to study in the neuroses. The term *unconscious*, which we have used in the purely descriptive sense before, now comes to imply something more. It designates not only latent ideas in general, but especially ideas with certain dynamic characters, ideas keeping apart from consciousness in spite of their intensity and activity" (262). This is the second meaning of the unconscious in Freud's vocabulary: *the dynamic unconscious*. This clearly suggests that the unconscious is not a function of repression or of repelling material from consciousness, but a product of the unsuitability of the material to enter consciousness. The suitability/unsuitability issue is what will guide us to the theory of the aconscious.

In the early stages of the psychoanalytic movement, until formulating the theory of sexuality in 1905, both defence and repression were interchangeable terms. Freud said (1914b): "I looked upon psychical splitting itself [creating a distance between consciousness and unconsciousness] as an effect of a process of repelling which then I called defence and later repression" (11). He used the term repression between 1906 and 1923 to connote both the process itself and the defence mechanism. During that period, and according to him, repression was: ". . . the cornerstone on which the whole structure of psychoanalysis rests" (1914b, 16). The reason is that the theory of catharsis is limited in regard to psychopathology to ". . . turning something away, and keeping it at a distance from consciousness" (1915b, 147). He kept hanging on to that thought relentlessly even when everything he discovered insightfully discredited it. In *The Ego and the Id*, Freud went back to that idea and modified it: "We must come upon something in the ego itself [resistance] which is also unconscious, which behaves exactly like the repressed" (1923, 17). Prior to that insight in the link between resistance (a manifestation of a defence) and the unconscious he found out that descriptively the repressed is not what constitute the etiology of the neuroses. He said later when he was consolidating his discovery (1915c): "let us state at the very outset that the repressed does not cover everything that is unconscious. The unconscious has a wider compass: the repressed are a part of the unconscious" (166).

Freud gradually became interested in the psychopathological processes more than the psychical mechanisms that "cause" them. The link between the object and the aim in the sexual *Trieb* replaced—in importance—the repressed sexual urge. Repression became merely one of the defence mechanisms. The paper "On Narcissism" did away with the libido theory, which was the main point in the cathartic theory and the main fabric of repression, hence the theory of catharsis was on the wane. The concept of narcissism was a turning point from *a theory of psychopathology based totally on symptomatology to finding the conception that could explain psychopathology; a conception that explains how a normal process could become abnormal.*

Point in fact; Freud's gradual shift from content to processes was marred by hesitations. He did not want to dump repression completely, his *pet* concept. He kept going back to the link between repression and the unconscious despite the obvious and necessary changes he made to the theory. In *The Ego and the Id* he reaffirmed that link by saying: "The repressed is the prototype of the unconscious to us" (1923, 15). Nevertheless he suddenly confirmed his uncertainties about that link and its cogency. When he began talking about resistance he quickly recognized that: ". . . the *Ucs.* does not coincide with the repressed . . . [t]hen we find ourselves thus confronted by *the necessity of postulating a third [unconscious], which is not repressed, we must admit that the characteristic of being unconscious begins to lose significance for us*" (my emphasis, ibid. 18).[6]

Although Freud discredited that link he still preserved it in a most strange way. In his second topography he changed the theory form of a topography of systems *Cs., Pcs.,* and *Ucs.* to a topography of psychical agencies *Ego, Id,* and *Superego*. Nevertheless, he retained the three systems and assigned mini-forms of them to all of three new agencies. Each agency in the new topography contained an old topographical structure within it. Thus, he allowed the dynamics of repression and the conflicts and forces to remain the core of the theory. This circuitous attempt to saving repression from oblivion brought out, in an unexpected way, the most specific and peculiar attribute of the unconscious as a system *Ucs*. *The systemic unconscious is the third meaning in Freud's vocabulary*. The ego (supposedly the agency of the conscious operations) "undoubtedly" contained unconscious attributes. He specifically characterized them as unconscious and not preconscious or merely latent.[7] He explained that idea saying: "A part of the ego too—and heaven knows how important a part—may be *Ucs*., undoubtedly is *Ucs.* (See Strachey footnote on this point). And this *Ucs*., belonging to the ego, is not latent like the *Pcs.*; for if it were, it could not be activated without becoming *Cs*. and the process of making conscious would not encounter such great difficulties" (ibid. 18). This phrase means that the unconscious part of the ego could be activated and it still remains unconscious, that is, a *non-repressed unconscious*.

At first, this idea looks blatantly paradoxical: thoughts that are present in consciousness but aconscious! To wit, it seems there is no link between repression and the aconscious, and what repression generates is not the aconscious. We seldom pay attention to many examples of unconscious psychical material that is adjectivally and dynamically not repressed. An ordinary person, even if uneducated, could speak his language with correct syntax and reasonable semantics and semiology, and could also notice the grammatical mistakes foreigners make in speaking his language, without being conscious of following any linguistic rules. Another example: Sophocles, for instance, was conscious of what he said in *Oedipus Rex*, but not fully conscious of the relation between the drama in his Oedipus and the human drama in general. Chomsky's idea of a "language faculty" and the surface structure vs. the deep structure in language illustrates this fact. Ordinary people are capable of making jokes or responding to them without any conscious analysis of the irony they comprise. As analysts we encounter in our daily practice the patient who intended consciously to say something and actually said it, yet without him being cognisant we realize that he also said something else.

At this juncture we can simply state that Freud had major difficulties in defining or understanding his most valuable discovery: the systemic unconscious, that is, the unrepressed unconscious. This difficulty was enough to have made him abandon that third and most significant meaning of unconsciousness, but he didn't though. He puzzled about it (see appendix A, in *The Ego and the Id*, and Strachey's weak explanation of Freud's puzzlement), yet *he left behind what could make us do what he could not do: have a theory of the aconscious.*

A THEORY FOR THE ACONSCIOUS

Freud discovered several aspects of the phenomenon of unconsciousness but did not put them in a unified comprehensive theory. It is fair to say that they were significant and profound intuitions, but they did not come in an identifiable sequence to recognize a consistent theoretical thread that strings them together. He tried something else to put those intuitions in some order, by discerning three distinct meanings of the term so each would be more expressive of one of its attributes. His three meanings of the unconscious are:

1. *Descriptively* unconscious is the *adjective* of the state of psychical material at the time it is not in consciousness. A temporary forgotten name or a phone number is descriptively speaking unconscious.

2. *Dynamically* unconscious is a *qualification* of the absence of psychical events from consciousness, having been present before (becomes preconscious, *Pcs.*). Forgetting the time to do something upsetting qualifies as unconscious because of *forces* standing in the way of the recall. This meaning of the concept deals with the forces that effects the change from present to absent, like the force of repression or displacement. It is unconscious in a state of dynamic instability that keeps the field of forgetting and recalling in a dynamic flux.

Those two meanings deal with conscious material that maintains their conscious attributes even when they are absent of consciousness. When absent they are in a state of precociousness, but when they return to consciousness they are back in the same condition they were before they were dynamically "unconscioused."

3. *Systemically* unconscious is a state of something that was not conscious at any time, and remains unconscious even when activated by other forces to get accesses to the *Pcs./Cs.* system. This unconscious is systemic in the sense that what is systemically unconscious is not subject to becoming conscious at any time or under any circumstance. Homeostatic changes are systemically unconscious but could generate representations to get them the chance to be communicated. Although representations of some psychicalogical nature, they still remain *aconscious,* for systemic reasons. Fantasies and representations generated by those changes are also aconscious because the primary process that turns them into fully fledged psychical material also happens aconsciously. They could link with material in the *Pcs.* and take secondary processes forms but have to abide by its rules to become conscious functions. This process demands being extensively worked out.

The systemic *Ucs.* in Freud's words is (1912): "The system [system unconscious] revealed by the sign that the single acts forming parts of it are unconscious . . . we designate by the name 'the unconscious,' for want of better and less ambiguous term. In German, I proposed to denote this system by the letters *Ubw, an abbreviation of the German word 'unbewusst.' And this is the third and most significant sense which the term unconscious has acquired in psychoanalysis*" (my emphasis, 266). With this definitive explanation Freud erased any vagueness regarding the difference between the *Pcs.*, and the *Ucs.* He underlined the difference by saying (1915c): ". . . the *system Pcs.* shares the characteristics of the system *Cs.* and that the rigorous censorship exercises its office at the point of transition from the *Ucs.* to the *Pcs.* (or *Cs.*)" (173). The systemic unconscious is distinct because structurally it does not call for repelling or expelling its content from consciousness. On the contrary, the endosomatic needs that are aconscious strive to get the means to enter consciousness so that it could get gratified.

However, Freud did not explicate fully or even partially the meaning of the systemic unconscious. The full extent of its meaning had to wait for two things to happen: A. The emergence of the structural theory[8] in epistemology, which was not yet fully configured at this time, and came later mainly in linguistics and anthropology. B. The interest in psychoanalysis by the intellectuals in the other fields of the humanities, especially those who adopted structuralism. The interest in psychoanalysis by the intellectuals started early in the twentieth century but mainly in its contribution to creativity. There was a slight curiosity about the workings of the unconscious in surrealism and the art of the absurd, but not in the *Ucs.* as a system. After the Second World

War, structuralism permeated the fields of the humanities. Some psychoanalysts, particularly in Europe, found a great advantage in putting the unconscious in the context of structuralism.

The interest in the systemic unconscious is most peculiar. The linguists, anthropologists, literary people, and artists had no interest in the dynamically unconscious (repressed content), and found their way easily in understanding the system *Ucs.*, and the structuring work of the primary process. Clinical psychoanalyst, on the other hand, bypassed all that and literarily ignored it and leaned toward ridding themselves of it. Clearly it was because they did not fully understand it (see Matte-Blanco, 1975). They were contented with the dynamic meaning only and even *declared* it "the official" unconscious of psychoanalysis (in a meeting of division 39 in Boston in the late nineteen nineties).

Now, as we have the full Freudian text well researched and indexed, we are capable of holding the theoretical thread of the unconscious and following it carefully to the systemic meaning of the term. The systemic unconscious has its start in the two papers on *The Neuro-psychosis of Defence* (1894, 1896 b). In those two early papers Freud came to a discerning observation about the link between affect (distinct from feeling) and its presentation. He realized from his clinical experience that the link between the explicates of affect and its implicates was arbitrary, random, and with no obvious correspondence between the nature of the affect and its representation in the mind, especially in neuroses. This arbitrariness creates a rift between what affects indicate and what they achieve. Better, Freud realized that what stimulates the mind to work (*Trieb*) does not in effect relate to its representations in a straightforward way.

Shortly after, and when he decided to abandon hypnosis, he realized that only through the circuitous characteristics of free association did we come to discover that link. This was the beginning of paying serious attention to the workings of the primary process, which he mentioned in the *Project*. The primary process, in this newly discovered field of mental functions, establishes the arbitrary link between the implicates and the explicates of the psychical phenomena.

In *The Interpretation of Dreams* (1900), Freud already had thorough knowledge of the working of the primary process. He referred the link between the manifest and the latent dreams to that working. The state of wishing as the source of the dream is worked up by the primary process to create a manifest dream that hardly reveals it. Because the wish is difficult to recognize in the manifest dream Freud considered it subject to *interpretation,* because the dreamer is unconscious of it, thus cannot contribute in expressing it. The manifest[9] had to be *interpreted* to get to the latent. He advanced that observation further to mean that the link between cause and effect are also arbitrary because the affect that generates the dream does not relate—in a straight line—to the thoughts that express it.

Freud specified three acts or results of working of the primary process: condensation or making a metaphor of the wish, displacement or making it a metonymy and what he called the plastic representation of ideas (a mixture of symbolism and concretizing an abstract). The primary process represents the affect metaphorically, metonymically or pictorially. Metaphors and metonymies cannot represent matters of conjunctions, like *if, and, maybe, but, etc.* The process of the plastic representation of ideas takes care of inserting a symbol that expresses a conjunction in a metonymy or a metaphor. The primary process could use its means to create those plastic representations. Freud, in examining dreams, showed that there is no concept for time but it is expressed by the sequence of events in the dream, and symptoms. Negation is another notion that has no place in the primary process so it is expressed by contradiction.

The unconscious had clear features: it is particular in using the part to represent the whole and visa-versa, or using a connotation as denotation, or using a concrete meaning as an abstract concept, or relating opposites without restriction, or having the present tense as the only time-frame (see Matte-Blanco 1975). The most important discovery about the unconscious is that the *Ucs.* is unpredictable in the way the primary process is going to work out its latent affect, or the manner in which the day residues (the *Pcs.*) will be attached to the infantile wish. Therefore, the method of dealing with psychical phenomena is interpretation to bring out the meaning of the aconscious.

In other words, Freud's discovery of the *Ucs.* responds to the three main difficulties neurologists faced in their matching between mind and brain: qualia, representation and subjectivity. *The systemic unconscious is what makes it possible for the subjective representation of the endosomatic need to have its individual value from the person, because of its potential to link a cause to its effect in no predictable ways.* For now we could say that the systemic unconscious is not rejectionable psychical content but the process that turns the subjective, the representational, into the quality of the consciousness of each individual.

Freud introduced the concept of *Trieb* in *The Three Essays on the Theory of Sexuality* (1905b). *Trieb* comprised a very important duality with two embedded links: the known link between the manifest expression of the *Trieb* and its meaning on one hand, and a link between its object and aim. The link between the manifest and latent in the *Trieb* is similar to the one encountered in dreams. However, the link of the object to the aim of the *Trieb* has a considerable impact on psychical life, because, though its qaulity is individualistic and specific of the person, it has lasting effect on him, that is, it is created by the subject but once it is created—and that happens unconsciously—it becomes him or identifies him. The link between the aim of the

Trieb (sucking) and the object (breast) is an open field for all possible variations of psychical manifestations (see the next chapter) and engenders very unexpected metaphors and metonymies.

When we consider that the links and their consequences are aconscious we could appreciate the significance of a theory of the unconscious in understanding consciousness. Since we are examining the important role *Trieb* plays in the formation of the aconscious we could skip the natural and historical progression of the concept to get to Freud's second *Triebhaft* set.

Freud's had two sets of *Trieben* in his theory of psychoanalysis; each set was a duality. The first set (1905b) was of *Ego-Trieb* (self-preservation) vs. *Sexual-Trieb* (preservation of the specie). The second set (1920) was *Life-Trieb* (anabolism) vs. *Death-Trieb* (catabolism). The link between life representations, like love, union, sexuality and their objects are clearly conditional on many factors that easily point at the impossibility of predicting the way the links would be established. Therefore we could add that the aconscious in humans is still an unexplored field of research. Although the originator of psychical life in the concept of *Trieb* came in the form of duality of opposed urges we cannot ignore that in both the dualities of ego/life and sex/death the urge for life was the basic endosomatic pole but without open behavioural manifestation, while sex and death were offshoots of that pole; as if they emanated from it.[10] In the final analysis we see that the working of the primary process is the rule of establishing the links between the dualities inherent in every psychological phenomenon.

We can go now to the notion of development in the theory of the unconscious. A few years after the presentation of the concept of *Trieb* Freud talked about the role of that duality in the formation of character neurosis (1908), and continued (1913) to describe the vicissitude of that duality in the *Trieb* as displacement of the object, and the sublimation of its aim. Unfortunately, Freud did not integrate his insight in the *book of dreams* with the rest of his insights that came with the *book of sexuality* (1905b) and what came after it. Integrating those insights would have defined the unconscious as the effort of the primary process to bridge the gap between affect and thought, the latent and the manifest dreams, the aim and the object of the *Trieb*, and the creator of the process of displacement and of sublimation. This way, the unconscious would have been freed from any link with repression. In spite of the scholars failing in emphasizing connections between Freud's insights, we cannot miss that he has left us a structural conception of the *Ucs.*, which is very different from the functional concept in the theory of repression of the unacceptable urges.

Primary process generates the representations of the endosomatic stimuli. With the features outlined about its working, and the absence of specialized organs that help in sorting out the source of the stimuli, representations do not submit to the working of the secondary process even after they link with the preconscious. They only latch to other psychical forms and link with them. The unfamiliar ways of the primary process require interpretation; they require getting something to talk about in the language of the secondary process. Without interpretation it will remain obscure and unintelligible. In the framework of the catharsis theory the working of the primary process is seen as *resistance* instead of realizing this new angle of the unconscious.

It is quite strange and significant that the scholars of Freud's text sidestepped totally the fact that primal repression of the *Trieb* was not to repress. On the contrary the *Triebhaft* urges seek a way to get to *consciousness*, but since it has no means of its own to become conscious or to move to the psychomotor system and change in behaviour,[11] the primary process manages to start the process of representation of it. In other words, primal repression forces the mind to represent the *Trieb*, thus releasing the endosomatic from its aconsciousness, turning it into mental quality, and allowing it, thus, to enter the realm of the ideational. The sign or the word belongs to the ideational realm. The sign, not the *Trieb,* becomes subject for repression proper. This distinction makes the *Ucs.*, a psychical structure of a specific nature, not linked to repression, and cannot be prototypical of it. Lemaire put it well saying: "Every repressed presentation, that is, may be conscious in that it is a term in the language of everyday life, and unconscious in that it is a conflictual element which goes in the interrelational network of the unconscious elements" (1977, 119).

This subtle but serious misunderstanding of the unconscious relates to discounting a Freudian insight—even by him—about the different qualities of the psychical material in the three systems of *Ucs.* and *Psc./Cs.* Freud made a distinction in the concept of representation (*Vorstellung*) between thing-presentation (*dingvorstellung*) and word-presentation (*Wortvorstellung*). The first presentation of an endosomatic stimulus is the object of that need (breast, feces, penis, etc.) which is what the mother offers as her interpretation of that need; the first representation is a thing. After numerous changes and representations of representations that *thing* acquires a sign and becomes a word. The word at the beginning is treated as a thing. The word as a representation of the thing would also go through a new chain of word replacements. However, when that intermediate stage has passed the world of language, then the network of meanings and symbols opens for the child to explore. Many things could happen to interfere with this developmental process. Some events could derail the progress or block it so progress remains fixated[12] at a certain point and the three systems do not function according to the movement *from endosomatic to thing presentation to word-thing presentation to word presentation to linguistic expression.*

Understanding primal repression this way presents us with a different prospect of the dilemma of the non-repressed unconscious. Primal repression gives *Trieb* the means to consciousness in the form of *representation.* The representation of the *Trieb* is some-*thing* that is not understandable to the infant of course, but also something the caregiver has to interpret, that is, it is not a verbal message to understand. The representation of the endosomatic stimulus is not repressed; nevertheless the child is not conscious of it and the caregiver is the one who will *give it* its conscious meaning externally. The non-repressed if not given a meaning will remain aconscious. Moreover, permitting the endosomatic to enter consciousness as representation enables it to link with preconscious material that is of a conscious nature, which takes the representation to consciousness from the back door, so to speak. Primal repression, in that sense, is what creates consciousness of the endosomatic, that is, consciousness as the first sign of the *self*. In examining dreams, symptoms, and parapraxes, Freud discovered that the unconscious is not the wish itself, which is unfailingly and always preconscious, but the signifier—the representation—of the wish which is not repressed. The wish therefore, could remain in consciousness or re-enter it, as long as its signifier remains aconscious.

There is a major difference between two sorts of consciousness: consciousness of the external world and consciousness of the self. The external world is known directly and it creates a one-step consciousness; it is a direct cognitive process. Consciousness of the self is different. The infant gets the meaning of the endosomatic, which is him himself, from the caregiver. The caregiver's proffered meaning is the prototype of any self-awareness that ensues. The self is always known through an external medium like the other or what the person has made-of-himself. Consciousness of the *self is never direct consciousness; it is at best a transcendental consciousness*. Clinically: ". . . the emergence of consciousness [of the self] occurs at the point of juncture between the interpretation of defence and the interpretation of transference" (Fayek 1980, 450). The systemic unconscious becomes meaningful when the person makes the effort to hide it and hedges it in a relationship with another in what could be called transference. This process is best revealed when transference as a defence mechanism fails to disguise it.

Lemaire explains this point in Lacan's thinking by saying: "Lacan's originality is to have wished to furnish proof that the signifier acts separately from its signification and without the subject being aware of it. 'It' (ca) [that] thinks in a place where it is impossible to say 'I am.' When that replaces 'I am' then, 'the unconscious becomes the discourse of the Other'" (1977, 38). The person feels then that someone else has made the slip of the tongue, so to speak, and exposed an aspect of him that was not intended to be revealed. In that regard, Freud said: "One should judge all acts and manifestations that I cannot link up with the rest of my mental life as belonging to another person" (1915c, 169).

It is a systemic unconscious that deceives and eludes consciousness through the intrinsic equivocality of language, which is not the familiar speech of consciousness. Matte-Blanco asked: "what makes us unconscious of the unconscious?" (1975). The answer is: we are unconscious of the unconscious because the endosomatic which is us cannot create consciousness of itself, or in the language of topographic metapsychology *it cannot enter consciousness without being changed into something mental.* That is done by a primary process that we—the infants—have no say about. This process takes off spontaneously and inevitably leads to the point where it links with the preconscious which is also partially unconscious. We will remain unconscious until someone interprets our behaviour, or an analyst comes to reveal it to us if we seek help.

NOTES

1. Damasio rejected the psychoanalytic concept of the unconscious on the basis that it meant repressed urges and rejectionable psychical contents.
2. Most probably Freud did not call the other repression secondary or sequel repression opting to calling it repression proper to maintain the original meaning of repression in the cathartic theory. It was to him the only repression; repression proper.
3. I mentioned before that Freud's concept of *periodicity* in neural transmission could be behind the process of representing the endosomatic stimuli. Kubie (1948) in his study of "*Instinct and Homeostasis*" stipulated that awareness of homeostatic change happens earlier than the real depletion of the vital substance (thirst comes long before complete dehydration), thus the pressure on the mind to react is not the same as when a beam of light irritates the eye. Could the difference in the increase of the instability in the case of the homeostasis create a different type of neural transmission?
4. The physical external stimuli are avoidable if they are not agreeable to the individual. However if the external psychological stimuli are a mother's reaction, there is no way to avoid them. The only possible reaction to an unacceptable external psychological stimulus is to deny it, which does not make it disappear but only forgotten.
5. Rain is a function of clouds, but both are the function of evaporation/condensation.
6. It would have been more logical for him to say: "the characteristic of being repressed begins to lose significance to us."
7. The ego (I) comprises the *Pcs./Cs.* systems by virtue of the predominance of the secondary process in their operation.
8. The structural theory has nothing to do with the "structural point of view" of the *Ego and the Id.*
9. The manifest is what we are conscious of, while its meaning is unconscious because even though it is possible to introduce it to consciousness it remains detached from the manifest if it did not come via interpreting it. Interpretation is the act that refers the meaning to its manifestation, thus consciousing it. Interpretation is the fabric of all human communication, and miscommunications.
10. It is more accurate to say that Freud had but only one set of *Trieben*: life and death (sexuality was included in the life *Trieb* in the last *Trieb* duality). Therefore, we have to concede that Freud's *Triebhaft* theory is of the endosomatic urge to live and the birth of its dialectical antithesis of death. Yet, we need to know how psychological life is the synthesis of those two poles of *Trieb*, because we know that psychical problems go wrong at the point when the transformation of one into the other takes place.
11. The human infant is incapable to respond behaviorally to his physical needs, and has to communicate them to the caregiver. The physical needs of the infant have to be transformed into something that is communicable and that happens when primal repression delays their gratification in search of the tools to communicate. Primal repression is the prerequisite for speech.

12. See Freud's statement on fixation (Freud 1915b, 148).

Chapter Six

The Unconscious and the Aconscious

Freud started in the *Project* by the idea that consciousness is a function of perception which is a function of the sensory organs, but he added that the external stimuli carry within them their qualitative distinctions. However, this "neat" identification of consciousness in those terms did not respond to consciousness of non-perceptive stimuli like thought processes, reasoning, memories, and verbal imagery. There was no other way for Freud to keep that proposed neat conception except by begging the question. He presumed that the non-perceptual stimuli have the capacity to turn into verbal entities, thus become perceptual in a roundabout way. Verbal recall, in his estimate, could have the attributes to attract attention. His conception of those links was influenced by his neurological mindset. When he advanced towards examining psychological life in general apart from neurology he made serious efforts to find a place for consciousness in his psychological theory. He tried that by formulating metapsychologies that would position consciousness within a total psychological framework.

Devoting most of his time to exploring the psychology of the psychoneurosis occupied him—at the beginning—with conscious material that was expelled from consciousness, yet its expulsion showed in certain and definite changes to consciousness. The changes were in the form of symptoms. In other words, repressing unacceptable conscious urges affect the rest of consciousness and create the neuroses, that is, neurosis is a distortion of consciousness. The result of his interest in repression drew his attention, in an unusual way, to problems with consciousness. The repressed always manage to create substitutes that occupy parts of consciousness, for example, symptoms, character disorders, interpersonal difficulties, and sometimes even physical symptoms. Better, part of consciousness could be repressed but it maintains its place in consciousness by other means. *Hence, he recognized that the unconscious is not the antithesis or opposite of consciousness,* because it also maintains a place among the rest of the conscious material.

This observation made him examine the unconscious differently. Most importantly and very significantly is paying attention to the ability of *reading* in the replacement of the repressed what was repressed. The repressed enters consciousness in a disguised manner; therefore we cannot say that it was erased completely. It is possible to discern between what is conscious and what is conscious but not in awareness. Therefore, understanding consciousness is a must and not a choice in the theory of the psychoanalysis.

Notwithstanding the validity of this argument, Freud came to the phenomenon of consciousness from a different angle, the angle that mystified serious thinkers before him, mystified him, and still puzzles thinkers until now. He was the first to engage in examining and making sense of the qualitatively unusual consciousness in psychopathological conditions. In actuality, he never dismissed anything unusual about consciousness as insignificant, but made every effort to understand it. Taking that attitude meant that the psychoneuroses create the distorted perceptions and conceptions of substantive matters, but the subject not the object is accountable for the qualia of his consciousness.[1] The most revealing part of this observation is that the distortions of consciousness vary depending on the kind of mental disorder the subjects suffer from. Thus, quale was not *the issue:* psychoneurosis is the issue. This is a double barrelled problem: If psychoneuroses produce qualitatively different consciousnesses, should we therefore conclude that in non-pathological conditions consciousness is expected to be the same in all normal or healthy people? That is not the case either, because "normals" still differ in their consciousnesses. Secondly, if the unconscious that is supposed to be the cause of psychoneuroses affects consciousness, even in normal people to a degree, then qualia is an inherent attribute of the human mind and a product of neither the brain nor the stimuli.

Freud tried early to consolidate his views about the psychopathology in the psychoneuroses and made some preliminary formulations about the nature of the unconscious in them (1894, 1896b). But, the progress of his work on psychopathology confronted him with the need to examine the human subject instead of his indicators. *Defining the human subject is the point of significance in psychoanalysis:* psychoanalysis is a theory of the human subject, in health and in sickness, conscious or unconscious, responding to his body and reacting to his external world, and most of all his ability and inclination to make the other conscious of his consciousness. If there is an implicit and unrecognized fact about the human subject it is an innate tendency to make his consciousness known, not through action but through linguistic actions or actions that have linguistic implications.

CONSCIOUSNESS IN METAPSYCHOLOGY

The individual differences in the nature of mental activities in humans—conscious/unconscious—do not find explanations in differences in brain anatomy and physiology. *Psychoneurosis, let alone that it is a specific, unique, and peculiar attribute of the human species, is one of the most recognizable areas of differences between humans in conscious activities.* Its existence is mostly, if not totally, manifested in peculiarities of conscious activities, whether mental or behavioural. The kind of consciousness each individual human has, normal or abnormal, strongly suggest that the human brain does not choose the mind that it will contain, but each particular person decides his own subjectivity,[2] the kind of qualia he adds to his perceptions and conceptions, and the nature of his representations of his endosomatic stimuli, for example, decides his specific personality and its idiosyncrasies.

As it happened, the *Project* turned out to be neurology for the psychologists, and not the other way around. Something similar happened when Freud worked on dreams. He mistakenly thought that his knowledge about the psychoneuroses would be helpful in dealing with the issue of dreams. However, Freud said (1900): "I have been unable to follow the historical development of my own views. Though my own line of approach to the subject of dreams was determined by my previous work on the psychology of the neuroses, I had not intended to make use of the latter as a basis of reference in the present work [*the book on dreams*]. Nevertheless . . . [I am] using dreams as a means of approach to the psychology of the neuroses" (ibid. 589). Point in fact: Freud is known as the discoverer of the unconscious, the psychopathology of the psychoneuroses, and the psychodynamics of mental abnormalities, when actually, he was discovering consciousness, and the functioning of the human mind, in both their normal and abnormal states.

As mentioned before, Freud considered affect with its pleasure/pain basis the originator of all psychical life, and called his theoretical formulation of the transformation of affect metapsychology. He has three metapsychologies that are *supposed* to contribute to normal psychology because they do not deal with any particulars of psychical activities, but reformulate psychical phenomena in terms of their structural attributes. The first metapsychology came round off the psychology of dreams, where he turned the discovery of the wishing into a general theory about psychical systems. A dream is the product of a state of wishing instigated the day before the dream, generating an affect (a preconscious state that the person could recall with some effort and identify what created the wish). The affect of the preconscious wish searches for a link with a childhood wish to create the dream. The childhood wish that is sought after is unconscious, but it is the main prototype of wishing since childhood. The preconscious affect is a variation of that prototype. The link between the wish of the dream (the day's residue) and the childhood wish is the work of the primary process; by which condensation and replacement construct the manifest dream while the latent content remains unfathomable. This link gives the preconscious wish the task of representing the combined unconscious and the preconscious wishes in a mental process similar to waking-life thinking.

Based on his conclusion that dreams are wishful-thinking Freud gave a metapsychology of that psychology in a definitive and even illustrative depiction of the psychical systems. The primary process manages the link between the unconscious system and the preconscious wish. This whole process is active while the person is asleep, which made Freud say: "The most that we can conclude from this is that it proves that the most complicated achievements of thought are possible without assistance of consciousness" (1900, 593). He is clear in considering a psychical operation to be constructed of several systems that interlink topographically (structurally) but are not incorporated. Each system of that apparatus could be functioning in conjunction with other systems and actively involved in the outcome, but separate and distinct. Although his depiction of the process of dreaming seemed conclusive, he gave hints to realize that it should not be a theory of dreaming but a general theory of psychoneuroses, and most probably a general theory of the psychical.

The first metapsychology—known as the topographic point of view—depicts three psychical systems, conscious, preconscious, and unconscious, which are *dynamically* creating psychical phenomena. The conscious in that topography was positioned next to perception and bordering the preconscious system on the other side. The point to underline before we go further is that Freud had established a framework that has two elements: a *psychical system* comprised psychical entities (and later psychical concepts) and *psychical processes* that oversees the interactions between those entities.

The topographic metapsychology raised few questions; two of them were: 1. What makes a wishful state seek a childhood wish to form a dream? Or create a symptom? 2. What makes the content of a system seek or accept a link with the content of another system? Those two issues forced Freud to compliment the topographic point of view with two other metapsychlogies: the *economical* point of view and the *dynamic* point of view. Freud invoked an *economic* point of view to talk about the unconscious as a permanent pressure imposing the strength of the affect on consciousness to be expressed. He also used the same concept of pressure to talk about the defence against the pressures of the unconscious. He resorted to use the conception of the two types of free and bound energy to explain how thoughts that acquire certain intensities manage to enter consciousness. The interplay between those forces were described in terms of a dynamic set up where tension and the release of tension decide the most adaptive balances between the conflicting forces.

The endeavor to give an economical depiction of the interplay of *forces* within the topographic metapsychology treated consciousness as an entity that has quantitative attributes. This was a necessary consideration to explain its invasion of the *Ucs.* of consciousness and the struggle of consciousness against that. The dynamic point of view dealt with the conflicts between the systems of *Cs., Pcs.*, and *Ucs.*, and the mechanism that would govern those conflicts. Freud puzzled at the fact that "the attributes of being conscious, which is the only characteristic of psychical processes that is directly presented to us, is in no way suited to serve as a criterion for differentiation between the systems. . . . Hence consciousness stands in no simple relation either to the different systems or repression" (1915c, 192). This statement, without any vagueness, assumes that the existence of consciousness and its separateness or independence of the other systems is problematic, even in a topographical conception of mental life. A scholar of the Freudian text would find a great difficulty in integrating the economic point of view and its dynamic extension in the topographic one, yet it seems that they all needed each other to make some sense.

Consciousness was a difficult subject to mold within the three metapsychologies. The place of consciousness in relation to the unconscious remained an unresolved problem in metapsychology; however, the need for metapsychology remained strong.[3] The reason is that Freud remained captive of the notion that the unconscious is repressed consciousness, thus they both share the same psychology and would not have different metapsychologies. If he had to have a metapsychology it should have been a metapsychology of repression, and not of consciousness or the other two systems.

Nevertheless, the topographic, the economic and the dynamic viewpoints offered a language that went beyond the psychical entities of metapsychology. Metapsychology facilitated explaining similar problems in other psychical processes in general. But most of all, metapsychologies furnished a conception of psychical life in which consciousness emerges from the unconscious, and the pathological emerges from the natural (not the normal). *It provided the vocabulary and grammar needed to talk about the variations and similarities, the permanent and the temporary, the usual and the unusual, the conscious and the unconscious, the banal and the original, health and sickness in the same language using the same grammar.* Better though, metapsychology is the language to use when talking about the human subject. The potential of metapsychology is the ease to speak of the distortion of the conscious caused by a psychopathology, using the same modality to speak about the difference between two psychoneuroses, or the different intensity of psychopathology in them. As an example Freud said (1900): "One of those factors devolves entirely upon the mental apparatus . . . while the other makes itself felt . . . and introduces instinctual forces . . . into mental life. Both of them originate in childhood" (603). Freud's metapsychologies shifted the emphasis to exploring the psychical processes and systems, instead of psychical entities. It is now possible to explain psychical phenomenon, like consciousness, within a framework.

As he assigned the function of perceiving the qualities of the quantitative changes in the stimuli to consciousness he should have expected the existence of two consciousnesses: one for the external stimuli and another for the qualities of the internal stimuli. Strangely but significantly, Freud instead suggested exactly the opposite: "two unconsciousnesses." He concluded that: "the unconscious (that is, the psychological) is found as a function of two separate systems and that this is the case in normal as well as in pathological life. Thus there are two kinds of unconscious, which have not yet been distinguished by psychologists. . . . [I]n our sense of one of them, which we term the *Ucs.* is also *inadmissible to consciousness*, while we term the other the *Pcs.* . . . are able to reach consciousness" (my emphasis, ibid. 614–615). To wit, when Freud came to specify two types of consciousness based on their source of stimulation he, somehow and without an obvious reason, shifted and talked about two kinds of unconsciousness.

This point remained an obscurity in Freud's dealings with the conscious (until the discovery of the *Project*). He did not follow the thread that *if consciousness is equivalent to perception then stimulation without sensory organs must create another type of consciousness, or another kind of perception*. Nonetheless, Freud came to correct himself later when he distinguished between three meanings of the unconscious (1915c) and assigned the adjective *systemic* to the unconscious, that is, the inadmissible material to consciousness, and designated italics to it: *Ucs.* It is an explicit admission that consciousness does not comprise only perceptual and cognitive entities, but it also consists of the entities of the systemic unconscious.[4]

For that reason, consciousness does have a place in metapsychology. Freud yielded and said: "The more we seek to win our way to a metapsychological view of mental life, the more we must learn to emancipate ourselves from the importance of the symptom of 'being conscious'" (ibid. 193). Consciousness as a separate system does not reveal what decides its relationship with the un-conscious or the pre-conscious. Better, the topographic point of view was supposed to start constructing a clear and defined framework for mental life, on the contrary, it reversed it and failed in providing coherent framework.

CONSCIOUSNESS AND THE TWO DETERMINING PSYCHICAL EVENTS

Metapsychology maintained the notion of distinct and separate entities of mental functions. But, Freud's practice of psychoanalysis obliged him to realize that in spite of the usefulness of the metapsychologies, the dynamics of mental functions are determined by developmental factors and individual psychological events that could not be included in any metapsychology. Those factors are extra-psychological events, related to the specific course of individual development.

The homeostatic condition of the human infant has an originary role in instigating awareness, which contributes in the emergence of consciousness; yet that contribution is completely silent and aconscious. The human infant's response to homeostatic changes is conditional on several factors that do not exist in the rest of the primates. The human infant is far less equipped to react to his endosomatic stimuli than the rest of the offspring of the other primates. The period and the degree of the infant's dependency on a caregiver in the human species is markedly greater than in any other species; and it is still extending with the advancement of civilization. The reactions of the caregivers to the needs of infants are very individualistic and are neither always consistent, nor available on demand. Shortly after birth the infant has to communicate his need in manners that establishes emotional ties with the caregiver; ties that get stronger and more complex over time, which is contrary to what happens with animals where those ties get less strong with the offspring's fast growing independence. Although there are innate commonalities between human infants—as in the rest of the animal kingdom—neither their expression nor the response to them is the same across the board.

The intense dynamic interaction between the human infant and the caregiver(s), and the endless possibilities in those interactions decides *two main things* about the emergence of consciousness in humans. The first is that endosomatic stimulation could only emerge in consciousness after getting mental representations. The construction of those representations is conditional on the dynamics of the infant/caregiver interaction. The caregiver, more than the infant, determines those representations (as we will see in the second psychical event). The infant's consciousness, which *is* the representation of the homeostatic changes in him, is the making of the caregiver. The infant's consciousness acquires its meaning externally, that is, he becomes conscious of what he was told of what he needs and feels. A psychological situation is thus created based on the particulars of the infant-mother relationship.

The endosomatic stimuli are the same in all infants, and will not change if the mother misreads them. If the infant is crying because he is tired and needs a nap and the mother offers him the breast as if he is hungry, that would not change the endosomatic stimulus. The endosomatic stimulus being misunderstood by the mother only gets distorted in the infant's mind. It does not take much to recognize that this process of representing the endosomatic stimulus in the infant's mind is an important psychical event. The chances of misconceptions and distortions are many, and will result in affecting the formation of consciousness in the infant. It is expected that there would be unconscious "feelings" (repressed) of frustration or pain in those events. Freud was very insightful as he said: "We then come to speak, in a condensed and not entirely correct manner, of 'unconscious feelings,' keeping up an analogy with unconscious ideas, which is not altogether justifiable. Actually the difference is that, whereas with *Ucs.* ideas connecting links must be created before they can be brought into *Cs.*, with feelings which are themselves transmitted directly this does not occur. . . . Even when they [feelings] are attached to word presentation, their becoming conscious is not due to that circumstance, but they become so directly" (Freud 1923, 22–23). This insight puts consciousness in a different perspective: the misrepresentation of the endosomatic stimulus in the mind would create a state of unfulfilled wish that pertains to that particular stimulus; this state forms an *unconscious affective* background to all the subject's consciousness. It becomes the source of fantasies, which over time establishes an unconscious mental attitude. At the same time, the feeling of that state of wishing would be linked to other elements in consciousness. This is—to a great extent—what Damasio called the *proto-self*. However, the proto-self is not created in the brain as he suggested; it is created in the relationship with the caregiver, consequently it rearranges the brain.[5] We could as well note here the original and fundamental gap in human consciousness that makes the individual *alienated* from himself, both in psychical health or sickness.

The second event is the process that decides the human infant's gaining of an identity. Gaining an identity is important if not vital to any sense of consciousness; because the individual has to take ownership of any consciousness he experience. If the individual is anything he is his body. Everything else about him is given or acquired. Thus, when the infant reacts to an endosomatic stimuli and his response is "expressed" he would be expressing *his-self*. As we noticed in the previous event, the caregiver will offer, if not impose, the representation of that self. The infant would always know himself through the other; a prototypal feature in any human self-awareness, healthy or pathological. As a result, a new psychological situation is created.

This second psychical event that has a fundamental role in the creation of consciousness is a two-step event. The infant has no sense of its being at the beginning, but gradually becomes aware of the caregiver's existence as an other. The *other* functions as a mirror to the infant's self: if the other is happy it is because he is good, and if unhappy it is because he is bad. The other at the beginning represents the child to himself. This self gets integrated in the unconscious affective background. Nonetheless, the infant will gradually become aware of the caregiver separate from the function of mirroring his image. A new and more complicated psychical situation is created in which the aconscious affective sense of being finds in the mirrored image a new consciousness of the self. This new consciousness is the consciousness of being a "*me*," the antithesis of "her/him." *Me* is a sense of being separate to an extent from the caregiver, and is an aconscious that becomes the core self in Damasio's terminology.

As the *me* takes its place in the relationship with the other, and the others, the infant enters the social network of "relations," which demands communication.[6] The *me* has to have a speaker who would express it to the other. The speaker for the *me* is the "*I*." The *I* is very much Damasio's autobiographical self. The *I* has the responsibility of expressing two unconscious entities and bring them to consciousness. Thus, it is an operation that exposes several previously mentioned problems with consciousness due to the fact that brains in the primates generate identical awarenesses in all the members of the same in the species, while in humans brains seem to indicate that they produce "made to measure" individual minds.

Consciousness emerges in the interaction between the infant and the caregiver for the reasons given above. In primates the interaction with the caregiver is the same all throughout the period of caring for the offspring, and is not different from a caregiver to another. In the human species, it is not possible to expect that a mother will respond to her toddler soiling his underwear the same way every time that happens. The same mother would respond differently to her fourth child when he has an accident. The variations in that regard show that consciousness about toilet training in children will decide how the brain will function. Moreover, the effect of those variations is not fixed and unchangeable. Both mother and child, and maybe a therapist in the future, could change that consciousness too. The plasticity of the human brain precludes the justification the functionalists gave to the function of the brain. However, that the subject's own personal experiences fashion his consciousness is not enough for the phenomenalists to obviate the role of the brain in putting together personal experiences in a conscious form.[7]

The three issues of representation, subjectivity, and qualia are more accessible to explanation in light of the individual experiences the subject acquires from his caregivers definition of his homeostatic, and the experiences that lead to identifying his *I*-ness. Those experiences are more demonstrative of the subject's consciousness when examined within the theory of psychopathology and psychotherapy in psychoanalysis.

The familiar theory of therapy in psychoanalysis has been and continued to reflect the basic premise of the catharsis theory, for example, *making the unconscious conscious.* This point of view is expressed well when Freud said: "for the dream is one of the roads along which consciousness can be reached by the psychical material which, on account of the opposition aroused by its content, has been cut off from consciousness and repressed" (1905c, 15). He even went as far as presuming the existence of a conscious counterpart to every unconscious thought (ibid. 55) as if every "upsetting" conscious idea would be repressed and would take a place in the unconscious. Even in the early simplistic conception of psychopathology and psychotherapy psychoanalysis was, in fact, a theory of consciousness in its different derivatives, varied forms, and individuality.

We cannot ignore that Freud had already discovered the primary process and the secondary process before instituting the sexual causality of repression and coining the maxim of making the unconscious conscious. He knew that what creates a pathological condition is the working of the primary process and not repression. He knew that there are components of the unconscious, which neither originate in consciousness and then gets repressed, nor remain unconscious due to the working of repression. He even stipulated that the unconscious is not the "thing" philosophers talk about but it is *a mental process* and that "conscious will-power governs only conscious mental processes, and every mental compulsion is rooted in the unconscious (1905a, 266). Therefore, the adage of making the unconscious conscious would not have had any clinical support at those early stages of formulating the theory, as they do not now. In the theory of psychopathology and psychotherapy a symptom or a character disorder is a conscious affair; the patient is conscious of it. Yet, he experiences it as a foreign aspect of himself. Better, a symptom seems to the subject to belong to someone else but he carries its burden. Therefore, explaining it to the subject changes nothing, because a symptom is consciousness but devoid of the patient's sense of its ownership. It is a representation of *his-self* but he does not recognize himself in it. At the same time, the symptom or the character disorder is a phenomenon that promises satisfaction, but somehow delivers that satisfaction to another latent self in the subject. Thus, the theory of psychopathology and psychotherapy in psychoanalysis uncovers and shows that the problem the analyst has to solve is not making the unconscious conscious but making the conscious understandable by interpreting its vagueness and elusiveness in the psychoneuroses. By doing that the patient could recognize himself in his symptoms and take ownership of his consciousness. This step is the basis of explaining the unexplainable consciousness in the neuroses.

The most important outcome of such understanding of the place of consciousness in psychoanalysis is realizing that not only people with psychopathology who are alienated from their consciousness but all human subjects are alienated of their consciousness in one way or another and in different degrees of alienation.

INTERPRETATION, METAPHOR AND METONYMY, AND CONSCIOUSNESS

The unexplainable consciousness in psychopathology is nevertheless *interpretable*. Ricoeur (1977) defined interpretation as the restoration of meaning or the demystification of illusions. Interpretation contrary to explanation does not *add* or expand consciousness, it changes it. However, we have to keep in mind that in psychoanalysis interpretation is a string of interpretations that restore, in a gradual way, the meaning of the unexplainable pathological consciousness or remove its obscurities. Interpretation as demystification of illusions or restoration of meanings works on consciousness—not on anything else. But it is imperative to explain how to interpret consciousness in the neuroses when it is not something that is understandable as is.

To recapitulate: consciousness in psychoanalysis starts from the pressure of the homeostasis on the mind (*Trieb*) to create mental representations that could relate to the caregiver or assimilate the representation offered by the caregiver. The representations create links between the endosomatic and the external world. Those links are the language of the psyche: there is no consciousness of the external world that is purely physical, as there is no consciousness of the self that is purely physiological. *Consciousness is structured as a synthesis of the endosomatic and the exosomatic*. This expression could be taken as another version of the embodiment of consciousness, but it is not. What it means is that the body remains aconscious all the time, as the external physical world exists and is also perceived all the time. But neither could be conscious material if it remains isolated. Food is an external object. If it does not get linked to hunger, which is its endosomatic corollary, it will never create the psychical "myth" that is woven around it. The myths about food come from the representation of hunger and its place in the symbolic order of the human subject. This is not the case in the rest of the animal kingdom where the homeostatic changes are also aconscious and instigate instinctual reaction. However, the external world remains in isolation of the endosomatic responses and never changes meaning. Lions hunt for food and do not go hunting for impalas one day and favor zebras the next. In humans the integration of hunger and food happens instantaneously at the source and results in preference and taste; a conscious discernment in the act of eating.[8] Without the integration of the endosomatic and exosomatic reactivity there would be no consciousness; that is, consciousness emerges from the integration of both functions and is not a result of their coexistence.

The emergent consciousness is a process that we come to only in its final configuration; after it is accomplished. Its accomplishment is manifested in the appearance of language indicating the state of consciousness. The very constituent of language in humans is translating meaning (what is conceived and understood) in audible or visual signs. It is not just sounds and gestures, but established sounds and gestures that carry meaning to the other. Jaynes says: "The most fascinating property of language is its capacity to make metaphors. . . . metaphor is . . . the very constitutive ground of language. . . . The grand and vigorous function of metaphor is the generation of new language as it is needed, as human culture becomes more and more complex" (1976, 48–49).

Lakoff and Johnson (1999) say: "Our unconscious conceptual system functions like a 'hidden hand' that shapes how we conceptualize all aspects of our experience. This hidden hand gives form to the metaphysics that is built in our ordinary conceptual systems" (13). It is only possible to integrate the endosomatic and exosomatic reactions if language has the means to allow that, because without those means each will have its own expressive ways when—supposedly—its expression has a complimentary aspect that is not included in the expression. Language has the means to preserve that integration. The final configuration of consciousness is the structuring of metaphors and metonymy.

Lakoff and Johnson said: "Metaphors and metonymy are different kinds of processes. Metaphor is principally a way of conceiving of one thing in terms of another, and its primary function is to understand. Metonymy, on the other hand, has primarily a referential function, that is, it allows us to use one entity to stand for another. . . . It also serves the function of providing understanding" (1980, 36). Lakoff and Johnson have shown in convincing ways that the modalities of our thinking, our language, our conception of the world around us, and our own identity are all "inframed" in bodily metaphors and metonymies. Our body gives meaning to objects and we assimilate those metaphors and metonymies unconsciously. When we say or hear someone saying: It is not in me to lie, or it is beyond me to understand what he has done, we are unconsciously accepting that the object which the subject is talking about resides in metaphors of the body. When we say he is the head of the family we all (even in other languages) know that he is oldest, the wisest, or the leader of the family.

Because what comes as conscious material is metaphorical or metonymical, whether in health or in sickness, there is always room for interpreting what is said. Freud offered a developmental model that became the foundation of the psychoanalytic system of psychopathology. He indicated that consciousness changes with age but could also get arrested at a certain stage of development; gets fixated. Fixation is maintaining certain features of consciousness of that stage and using it in configuring matters in another stage. The person could develop beyond his point of fixation but his consciousness remains captive of that point. Fixation on the oral phase makes the representation of hunger with emptiness and satiation with fullness a metaphor of all the deprivations and fulfillment in the other phases of development. In other words, the experiences in any developmental stage would create its metaphors and metonymies (in representations) and the patient's fixation would come through his consciousness in the forms of those metaphors and metonymies.

Interpreting what the subject talks about is relating his metaphorical and metonymical operations to the links between the endosomatic and the exosomatic. Interpretation changes consciousness by inducing the meaning of its metaphors and metonymies and including it in the subject's consciousness. The restoration of the meaning by interpretation closes the gap between the cause and the effect of the symptom. Interpreting a sense of disappointment in the analyst could reveal its origin in a previous disappointment in a parental figure. Revealing that link demystifies the illusion that the analyst is below expectation and could show that expecting more from him is the cause of disillusionment. Interpretation changes consciousness from the falsity of the now to the truth of the then.

Consciousness to the analyst is a measure of the patient's condition and something to change by the act of interpretation. It is the analyst's window on the aconscious. Nevertheless, if we agree with Freud's conception of the splitting of mental life into the three separate entities we would not be giving consciousness its proper place in psychoanalysis. Consciousness in psychoanalysis is in the context of the theory of the unconscious.

NOTES

1. The earliest step Freud took towards a psychological theory was by linking consciousness to perception calling it "perception-consciousness." He held the view that perception receives *perceptive qualities* weaves into the stimuli. He said (1950): "Consciousness gives us what are called *qualities*—sensations which are *different* in a great multiplicity of ways and whose *difference* is distinguished according to its relations with the external world. Within this difference there are series, similarities and so on, but there are in fact no quantities" (308). This starting point proved to be too simplistic when he began a serious examination of consciousness in psychoneuroses.

2. This statement looks metaphysical, because it offers a non-physical source of the mind and rejects a physical one. However, the notion of the brain as the explanation of the mind has proven to be materially insufficient. The person's conscious and unconscious formation of his own mind is far from being studied enough to be qualified or disqualified. Freud was the first to delve into its complexities. Nevertheless, he too was tempted to look at the mind as a marker of the individual and not the other way around. He did not want to venture and speculate about something in humans that makes them make their brains function individually.

3. Freud expressed that need by saying in his last work (1940) : "Without metapsychological speculation—I almost said 'phantasying'—we shall not get another step forward" (225).

4. Most of the work done on the unconscious after the theory of dreams was hovering around three main notions embedded in Freud's thinking. The first is that the *Cs.* and the *Pcs.* are incapable of creating a true psychical entity without a contribution from the *Ucs.* He said: "Thought-processes are in themselves without quality, except for the pleasurable and unpleasurable excitations which accompany them. . . . In order that thought-processes may acquire quality they are associated in human being with verbal memories . . . whose residues of quality . . . draw attention of consciousness" (1900, 617). The second notion is that normal thought is subject to abnormality when an unconscious wish invades consciousness. The third

notion is that there is no gradation between the systems *Cs., Pc.,* and *Ucs.*, that is, they are separate entities within the framework of the psychical phenomena.

5. Damasio does not ignore or deny that the human brain constantly restructures itself due to its plasticity and malleability to rearrangement. It rearranges itself based on the subject's experiences and mapping those experiences. Because those experiences in the human species are dependent on the other(s) it could be safely said that the self rearranges the brain.

6. Animals communicate by different means depending on their instinctual endowments. In the primates we notice increasing reliance on sound signals that are limited compared to human usage of sound (vocal) in communicating. The reason (the immediate explanation) is the wide range of subjects that humans need to communicate about. This is a question for the field of language: did our extensive needs make us change our brains to allow us to talk, or did the existence of language regions in our brains give us that advantage to widen the scope of what we communicate about?

7. There is an aspect of consciousness in humans that is seldom brought up in any discussion about it as a phenomenon. Consciousness in animal is stunted and does not evolve, because genetic mutations have already brought about the homo-sapiens species. Intelligence in gorillas is the same for the last few million years since it branched out from the baboon species. Consciousness in humans has evolved and is still evolving. Furthermore, there are signs that the advancement of consciousness in the human species is cumulative and not only a result of storing information but possibly of storing the information in writing. This is possibly another aspect of the same genetic mutation that distinguished the homo-sapiens. In recent studies of IQ in sample schools around the world students in advances societies have gained five points in their intelligence quotient over the last thirty years.

8. Julian Jaynes (1976) has a theory about the emergence of consciousness in humans that stipulates integration of the left and right sides of the brain resulting, in the integration of aspects of psychical life that are not very different from the conscious and the unconscious mental processes.

Bibliography

Anthony, M. 2002. "Concept of consciousness, kinds of consciousness, meaning of consciousness." *Philosophical Studies* 109: 1–16.

Antognazza, M. E. 2009. *Leibniz: An Intellectual Biography*. Cambridge: Cambridge University Press.

Becerra, R. 2004. "Homonymous mistakes with ontological aspirations: the persisting problem with the word 'consciousness.'" *Sorites* 15: 11–23.

Bickard, M. H. 2005. "Consciousness and reflective consciousness." *Philosophical Psychology* 18: 205–218.

Blackmore, S. 2005. *Consciousness: A Very Short Introduction*. Oxford-New York: Oxford University Press.

Brentano, F. 1929. *Sensory and Noetic Consciousness: Psychology from an Empirical Standpoint III*. Edited by O. Kraus and L. McAlister (English Edition) and translated by M. Schattle & J. McAlister. London: Routledge & Kegan Paul.

Chemero, A. 2011. *Radical Embodied Cognitive Science*. Cambridge, Massachusetts-London: The MIT Press.

Copleston, F. 1993. *Modern Philosophy from Descartes to Leibniz*. New York: Doubleday.

Combs, A. 2009. *Consciousness Explained Better*. St. Paul, Minnesota: Paragon House.

Damasio, A. 1999. *The Feeling of what Happens: Body and Emotion in the Making of Consciousness*. San Diego-New York-London: Harvest Book Harcourt.

Damasio, A. 2004. "The Neurology of Feeling." Keynote Address, 43rd Congress, New Orleans, LA, July 2004.

Damasio, A. 2012. *Self Comes to Mind*. New York: Random House, Inc.

Dennett, D. 1983. "International systems in cognitive ethology: the 'Panglossian paradigm' defended." *Behavioral and Brain Sciences* 6: 343–390.

Dennett, P. 1991. *Consciousness Explained*. Boston: Little Brown.

Denton, M. 1986. *Evolution: A Theory in Crisis*. Chevy Chase, Maryland: Adler & Adler.

Descartes, R. 2000. *Meditations and other Metaphysical Writings*. Translated by D. M. Clarke. London: Penguin Classics.

Edelman, G. M. and G. Tononi. 2001. *A Universe of Consciousness: How Matter Becomes Imagination*. New York: Basic Books.

Edwards, R. 1972. *Encyclopedia of Philosophy*. New York: Macmillan Colliers.

Fayek, A. 1980. "From interpretation to the death instinct." *International Review of Psychoanalysis* 7: 447–457.

Fayek, A. 2013. *Freud's Other Theory of Psychoanalysis: The Replacement of the Indelible Theory of Catharsis*. New York: Jason Aronson.

Ford, C. D. 1963. *Habitat, Economy, and Society*. London: Mathuen.

Freud, S. 1894. "The neuro-psychoses of defence." In *The Standard Edition* 3: 41–61. London: Hogarth Press.

Freud, S. 1895a. "Letter, April 27, 1895." In *The complete letters of Sigmund Freud to Wilhelm Fliess, 1887–1904*. Edited and translated by J. Masson. Cambridge-London: The Belknap Press of Harvard University Press.

Freud, S. 1895b. "Letter, May 25, 1895." *The complete letters of Sigmund Freud to Wilhelm Fliess, 1887–1904*. Edited and translated by J. Masson. Cambridge-London: The Belknap Press of Harvard University Press.

Freud, S. 1895c. "Letter, October 20, 1895." *The complete letters of Sigmund Freud to Wilhelm Fliess, 1887–1904*. Edited and translated by J. Masson. Cambridge-London: The Belknap Press of Harvard University Press.

Freud, S. 1895d. "Letter, November 8, 1895." *The complete letters of Sigmund Freud to Wilhelm Fliess, 1887–1904*. Edited and translated by J. Masson. Cambridge-London: The Belknap Press of Harvard University Press.

Freud, S. 1896a. "Letter, December 6, 1896." *The complete letters of Sigmund Freud to Wilhelm Fliess, 1887–1904*. Edited and translated by J. Masson. Cambridge-London: The Belknap Press of Harvard University Press.

Freud, S. 1896b. "Further remarks on the neuro-psychosis of defence." In *The Standard Edition* 3: 379–403.

Freud, S. 1897. "Draft M. May 25, 1897." *The complete letters of Sigmund Freud to Wilhelm Fliess, 1887–1904*. Edited and translated by J. Masson. Cambridge-London: The Belknap Press of Harvard University Press.

Freud, S. 1899. "Letter, January 3–4." *The complete letters of Sigmund Freud to Wilhelm Fliess, 1887–1904*. Edited and translated by J. Masson. Cambridge-London: The Belknap Press of Harvard University Press.

Freud, S. 1900. *The Interpretation of Dreams*. In *The Standard Edition* Vol. 4–5. London: Hogarth Press.

Freud, S. 1905a. "On Psychotherapy." In *The Standard Edition* 7: 255–268. London: Hogarth Press.

Freud, S. 1905b. *Three Essays on the Theory of Sexuality*. In *The Standard Edition* 7: 133– 243. London: Hogarth Press.

Freud, S. 1905c. "Fragments of an Analysis of a Case of Hysteria." In *The Standard Edition* 7: 1–122. London: Hogarth Press.

Freud, S. 1908. "Character and Anal Eroticism." In *The Standard Edition* 9: 167–176. London: Hogarth Press.

Freud, S. 1912. "A Note on the unconscious in psychoanalysis." In *The Standard Edition* 12: 255–266. London: Hogarth Press.

Freud, S. 1913. "The disposition to obsessional neurosis." In *The Standard Edition* 12: 311–326. London: Hogarth Press.

Freud, S. 1914a. "On Narcissism: An Introduction." In *The Standard Edition* 14:67–104. London: Hogarth Press.

Freud, S. 1914b. "On the history of psychoanalysis." In *The Standard Edition* 14: 7–66. London: Hogarth Press.

Freud, S. 1915a. "Instincts and Their Vicissitudes." In *The Standard Edition* 14: 109–140. London: Hogarth Press.

Freud, S. 1915b. "Repression." In *The Standard Edition* 14: 146–158. London: Hogarth Press

Freud, S. 1915c. "The Unconscious." *The Standard Edition* 14: 166–204. London: Hogarth Press.

Freud, S. 1917. "A difficulty in the path of psycho-analysis." In *The Standard Edition* 17: 135–144. London: Hogarth Press.

Freud, S. 1918. "From the history of an infantile neurosis." In *The Standard Edition* 17: 1– 122. London: Hogarth Press.

Freud, S. 1920. *Beyond the Pleasure Principle*. In *The Standard Edition* 18: 64. London: Hogarth Press.

Freud, S. 1923. *The Ego and the Id*. In *The Standard Edition* 19: 13–68. London: Hogarth Press.

Freud, S. 1926. "The question of lay analysis." In *The Standard Edition* 20: 177–250. London: Hogarth Press.

Freud, S. 1940. *An Outline of Psychoanalysis*. In *The Standard Edition* 23: 144–207. London: Hogarth Press.

Freud, S. 1950. "A project for a scientific psychology." In *The Standard Edition* 1: 283–397. London: Hogarth Press.

Gilson, E. 1991. *The Spirit of Medieval Philosophy*. Indianapolis, Indiana: Notre Dame University Press.

Gottlieb, A. 2002. *The Dream of Reason: A History of Western Philosophy from the Greeks to the Renaissance*. London-New York: Norton & Company.

Henrdich, T. 2005. *The Oxford Companion to Philosophy*. Oxford: Oxford University Press.

Jaynes, J. 1976. *The Origin of Consciousness in the Breakdown of the Bicameral Mind*. Boston: Houghton Mifflin Company.

Johnson, D. M. 2003. *How History Made the Mind: The Cultural Origins of Objective Thinking*. LaSalle, Illinois: Open Court.

Jones, E. 1954. *Sigmund Freud: Life and Work*. London: Hogarth Press.

Kubie, L. 1948. "Instincts and Homeostasis." *Psychosomatic Medicine* 10: 8–15.

Lakoff, G., and M. Johnson. 1980. *Metaphors We Live By*. Chicago: The University of Chicago Press.

Lakoff, G., and M. Johnson. 1999. *Philosophy in the Flesh, The Embodied Mind and its Challenge to Western Thought*. New York: Perseus Books Group.

Laplanche, J. 1976. *Life and Death in Psychoanalysis*. Translated by J. Mehlman. Baltimore-London: John Hopkins University Press. First published 1970.

Laplanche, J., and J. B. Pontalis. 1973. *The Language of Psychoanalysis*. Translated by Donald Nicholson-Smith. New York: Norton.

Larmand, D. 1996. "Nonphenomenal consciousness." *Nous* 30: 242–261.

Lemaire, A. 1977. *Jacques Lacan* (D. Macey Trans.). London: Routledge and Kegan Paul.

Limnatis, N. 2008. *German Idealism and the Problem of Knowledge: Kant, Fichte, Schelling, and Hegel*. Springer, the Netherlands: University of Amsterdam.

Matte-Blanco, I. 1975. *The Unconscious as Infinite Sets: An Essay in Bi-Logic*. London: Duckworth.

Mehlman, J. 1976. Introduction to *Life and Death in Psychoanalysis* by J. Laplanche. Translated by J. Mehlman. Baltimore: John Hopkins University Press.

Opatow, B. 1997. "The real unconscious: psychoanalysis as a theory of consciousness." *Journal of American Psychoanalytic Association* 45: 865–890.

Politzer, G. 1994. *Critique of the Foundations of Psychology*. Translated by A. Appry. Pittsburgh: Duquesne University Press. First published 1928.

Pribram, K. H., and M. M. Gill. 1976. *Freud's Project Re-Assessed*. New York: Basic Books.

Reboul, A. 2012. "Radical embodied cognition vs. 'classical' embodied neuroscience." In *Cognition and Embodiment*, edited by Z. Yu. Shanghai: University Press.

Reese, W. L. 1999. *Dictionary of Philosophy and Religion*. Amherst, New York: Humanity Books.

Ricoeur, P. 1977. *Freud, and Philosophy: An Essay on Interpretation*. Translated by D. Savage. New Haven: Yale University Press.

Russell, B. 1964. *Problems of Philosophy*. Oxford: Oxford University Press.

Russell, B. 1967. *History of Western Philosophy*. Canada: Simon & Schuster Touchstone.

Saunders, J. 1997. *Greek and Roman Philosophy after Aristotle: Readings in the History of Philosophy*. New Jersey: Free Press.

Schopenhauer, A. 1995. *The World as Will and Idea* (Abridged). Edited by D. Berman and translated by J. Berman. New York: Everyman's Library.

Sheets-Johnstone, M. 1998. "Consciousness: A natural history." *Journal of Consciousness Studies* 5: 260–294.

Sherrington, C. 1906. *The Integrative Action of the Nervous System*. New York: Charles Scribner's and Sons.

Solomon, R., and K. Higgins. 1996. *A Short History of Philosophy*, Oxford: Oxford University Press.

de Sousa, R. 2002. "Twelve varieties of subjectivity: Dividing in hopes of conquest." *Knowledge, Language, and Representation* May 15.

Sperry, W. 1975. "In search of psyche." In *The Neurosciences: Paths of Discovery*. Edited by F. G. Worden, J. P. Swazey, and G. Adelman. Cambridge, Massachusetts: MIT Press.

Strachey, J. 1950. "Editor's Introduction: Project for a Scientific Psychology." In *The Standard Edition* 1: 283–293. London: Hogarth Press.

Velmans, M. 2009. "How to define consciousness—and how not to define consciousness." *Journal of Consciousness Studies* 16: 139–156.

Wilson, M. 2002. "Six views of embodied cognition." *Psychonomic Bulletin & Review* 9: 625–636.

Wundt, W. 1878. *An Introduction to Psychology*. Translated by R. Pinter. London: Allen & Unwin.

Index

About the Author

Ahmed Fayek, PhD, is a retired clinical psychologist as well as a retired training and supervising psychoanalyst. Before his retirement he was a member of the International Psychoanalytic Society, the Canadian Psychoanalytic Society and Institute. Presently he is a member of the American Psychoanalytic Association. He was Associate Professor of clinical psychology in his country of origin, Egypt. In Canada, he was the head of the departments of psychology at St. Mary's Hospital and the Royal Ottawa Hospital. He trained in psychoanalysis in Egypt and another time at the Canadian Institute of Psychoanalysis in Montreal. He has published both in Arabic and in English, with works translated into German and French. This book is his fourth in English.

CPSIA information can be obtained at www.ICGtesting.com
Printed in the USA
BVOW07*1616020914

364958BV00002B/2/P

9 781442 242500